OCCUPY THE FU

OCCUPY THE FUTURE

edited by David B. Grusky,
Doug McAdam, Rob Reich,
and Debra Satz

A Boston Review Book

THE MIT PRESS Cambridge, Mass. London, England

MIT Press books may be purchased at special quantity discounts
for business or sales promotional use. For information, please
email special_sales@mitpress.mit.edu or write to Special Sales
Department, The MIT Press, 55 Hayward Street, Cambridge, MA
02142.

This book was set in Adobe Garamond by *Boston Review*
and was printed on recycled paper and bound in the United States
of America.

Library of Congress Cataloging-in-Publication Data

Occupy the future / edited by David B. Grusky ... [et al.].
    p.   cm. — (Boston review books)
ISBN 978-0-262-01840-1 (hbk. : alk. paper)
1. Income distribution—United States. 2. Equality—United
States. 3. Poverty—United States. 4. United States—
Economic conditions—2009– 5. United States—Social
conditions—2009– I. Grusky, David B.
HC110.I5O266 2013
339.20973—dc23

                                    2012038436

10   9   8   7   6   5   4   3   2   1

For our children:
  Max and Dash, Taylor and Molly,
  Gus and Greta, and Isaac

"*True compassion is more than flinging a coin to a beggar; it comes to see that an edifice which produces beggars needs restructuring.*"
            –*Martin Luther King, Jr.*

"*It is justice, not charity, that is wanting in the world.*"
            –*Mary Wollstonecraft Shelley*

CONTENTS

I

Introduction

Occupy the Future

David B. Grusky, Doug McAdam, Rob Reich, and Debra Satz

IN LATE SEPTEMBER OF 2011, THE OCCUPY WALL Street protest in Zuccotti Park began attracting national and international media attention. By late October, without any evident coordination, Occupy protests began appearing in scores of other cities and in many other countries. What looked at first like a burst of outrage at Wall Street and the irresponsibility of global financial institutions became a more general and sustained protest against historic levels of inequality and, in particular, the rising share of national income controlled by a tiny sliver, the so-called 1 percent.

"We are the 99 percent" became the slogan of the protesters, a capacious and inspired banner that permitted a large group to air diverse grievances. In the fall and earlier winter of 2011, the Occupy protests spread in ways that invited some to speculate that they might ultimately develop into a "social rights" movement with all the reach, power, and influence of the civil rights movement of the mid-twentieth century. Given how quickly the movement withered in the wake of the forced closures of the encampments in early 2012, these early optimistic assessments now appear premature, if not downright naïve. But movements are subject to unpredictable ebbs and flows. We would do well to remember that even the civil rights movement did not advance linearly. After the high water mark of the Montgomery Bus Boycott in 1956, the movement struggled to find its footing and was largely moribund before the lunch counter sit-ins revitalized it in the spring of 1960.

What becomes of the Occupy movement will depend not just on external events of this sort but also whether those who identify with the movement can fashion a compelling narrative that reenergizes protest around the issue of inequality. Given that the United States has historically been quite tolerant of inequality, it's not enough to proclaim that inequality has suddenly become too high. What, precisely, makes it *too* high? Don't we need to consider *how* so much inequality has been generated? Don't we need to examine the consequences of rising inequality for other outcomes that we cherish, such as opportunities for political expression? Don't we need to think carefully about the types and forms of inequality that are and aren't legitimate? The simple agenda behind this book is to take on these and related questions and thereby begin to develop a far-reaching and resonant narrative.

The backdrop to our effort is an Occupy-inspired teach-in at Stanford University on December 9, 2011. The faculty and students involved in this teach-in, including the editors of this book, were sympathetic to Occupy's complaints about inequality. Indeed many of them had devoted their scholarly lives to addressing issues of inequality, only to find that the world suddenly cared about what had heretofore been a largely academic area of inquiry. The key question on our minds at the time was whether the Occupy protests warranted our full support and participation. We understood, in other words, what Occupy was against, but what was it for? This question motivated us to describe how and why gaping inequalities have emerged and to lay out what's troubling about those inequalities.

As preparation for the teach-in at Stanford, a distinguished group of Stanford professors agreed to write short opinion pieces about the Occupy protests. These articles, published in an online forum in *Boston Review*, reflected the varied backgrounds of the scholars by addressing such diverse issues as the institutional sources of rising inequality, the influence of money in politics, the declining access to education, and the role of art in social change. After the teach-in, we asked the contributors to expand their short pieces into short chapters, and this book is the result.

In expanding their essays, we asked the contributors not to examine Occupy as if it were an object of scholarly study, an already dead specimen awaiting a dispassionate and disciplined autopsy. This book is not an analysis of Occupy as a protest or movement; it's not an effort to understand its roots or organization; and it's not a reflection on its prospects. This book is intended, rather, to offer a broader framework for understanding why rising inequality is the core problem of our time.

In short, this is a book with an agenda, an Occupy-friendly agenda. Nonetheless, the authors of most of the chapters were asked to carefully ground their opinions in data of unimpeachable quality and provenance.

The resulting book is most surely not a manifesto. The contributors should not be understood to endorse the contents of every chapter. The closest we come to consensus is our commitment to a vision of the United States as a country deeply committed to the principles laid out in our founding documents and upheld by a succession of leaders of every political party. We believe that everyone, not just the rich, should have the opportunity to get ahead or otherwise lead a good life. We believe that everyone, not just the rich, should have a right to be heard when our country makes decisions about its future. And we believe that everyone, not just the rich, should have an opportunity to participate fully and meaningfully in society.

We don't always live up to our most cherished ideals. Our country's history has been driven instead by a tension between our principles and our practices. Now and then, the disjuncture between our ideals and institutions has been exposed and led to dramatic reform. We've ended slavery. We've extended the franchise to women. And we've secured basic civil rights for all. Some of these projects remain works in progress. But the defining feature of our country is our commitment to making our most cherished principles real and meaningful rather than hollow.

The foregoing commitment plays out in five sections. The opening section offers an empirical examination of inequality in the United States and a normative examination of what kinds of inequality are morally objectionable.

The remaining sections take up different aspects of inequality: the sources of rising inequality; who bears the brunt of the effect; the relationship between inequality, politics, and democracy; and finally the costs of inequality for the environment, health, culture, and the arts.

Throughout these essays, we link criticism of inequality to the aspirations embedded in American founding principles and in the American Dream. Are we entering another moment in history in which the disjuncture between our principles and our institutions is being cast into especially sharp relief? Are new developments, such as the rise of extreme inequality, opening up new threats to realizing our most cherished principles? Can we build an open, democratic, *and* successful movement to realize our ideals?

II

The Empirical and Normative Foundation

Economic Inequality in the United States:
An Occupy-Inspired Primer

David B. Grusky and Erin Cumberworth

THE IDEA THAT INEQUALITY IS A MAJOR SOCIAL problem in the United States was once a niche belief limited to hard-core leftists, socialists, and Marxists. Why, they asked, is the American public so tolerant of the extreme inequality in its midst? When would middle-class voters come to their senses and stop backing the political party that was generating so much inequality?

But that was then. We now live in a world in which mainstream journalists and the informed public are also openly worried about inequality.

Figure 1. References to "inequality" in U.S. news

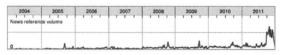

Source: Google analytics (accessed Jan. 5, 2012)

This newfound public concern about inequality has precipitated much journalism and commentary about the state of inequality in the United States. The purpose of our chapter is to ground this new public conversation about inequality in data of unassailable quality. We present here the best available data on four key questions:

• Is there much income and wealth inequality in the United States?

• Has there been a rapid increase in income and wealth inequality in the United States?

• Is the United States distinctively unequal?

• What are the main forces behind any changes in income inequality?

How Much Inequality Is There?

We begin with a simple figure conveying the extent of income and wealth inequality in the contemporary

United States. In measuring income inequality, we've presented data from the non-partisan Congressional Budget Office (CBO), which draws on Internal Revenue Service (IRS) tax returns and the Current Population Survey (CPS) to measure inequality in real (i.e., inflation-adjusted) household income after government transfers and federal taxes. This is a conservative measure in the sense that it pertains to inequality *after* the redistributive effects of taxes and transfers are allowed.[1] Elsewhere in this chapter, we will also refer to measures of "market income," where that pertains to the sum of all income sources before taxes are assessed and transfers (e.g., unemployment benefits) are counted. Because taxes and transfers have a progressive (i.e., inequality-reducing) effect, the estimates of Figure 2 will reveal less inequality than those based on market income.[2]

The CBO estimates, however "conservative" they may be, nonetheless reveal much inequality. In Figure 2, it's shown that only 4.9 percent of the national income goes to the lowest quintile, while a full 52.5

Figure 2. Shares of national income and wealth by quintile

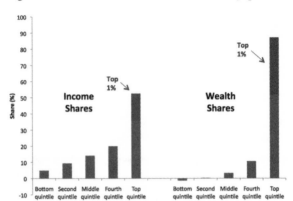

Source: Income data are from the Congressional Budget Office; wealth data are from the Economic Policy Institute

percent goes to the top quintile. It follows that the top quintile has an average income 10.7 times greater than that of the bottom quintile. As for the now-famous one percent, the CBO data indicate that, after taxes and transfers are taken into account, it controls a full 17.1 percent of the national income.

The right side of Figure 2 pertains to wealth inequality in 2009. These data, which are based on the Survey of Consumer Finances (SCF), pertain to the total assets of households after subtracting their total liabilities (i.e., "average net worth").[3] The wealth distribution is shown here to be exceedingly skewed. The top quintile, for example, takes 87.2 percent of the nation's wealth, a share that's far higher than its income share. The top one percent is further shown to control over a third of the nation's wealth (i.e., 35.6 percent). At the same time, the bottom quintile of households has negative wealth (i.e., liabilities exceed assets), while the second quintile has a mere 0.3 percent share. The simple conclusion: The bottom 40 percent of households is effectively without any wealth at all.

What should one make of these results? The conventional characterization, and indeed we've already lapsed into it, is to label the results of Figure 2 as revealing "much inequality." On what basis, however, does one come to the conclusion that there is *much* inequality? In the end, that type of judgment must of course be grounded in a comparison, a comparison that may be carried out in terms of (a) what prevailed in the past, (b) what prevails in other countries, or (c) what prevails in some ideal-typical world. Although we will attempt comparisons of all three types in the following sections, we will be focusing mainly on the first two types. In the next chapter of this book, Rob Reich and Debra Satz will address the third type of judgment in far more detail, hence it's unnecessary to attempt any protracted discussion of it here.

Trends In Inequality

We lead off our comparative analysis by considering trends in income inequality in the United States. Because we're interested in trends over the very long term, our best source is the Internal Revenue Service (IRS) tax return data, and our time series will accordingly pertain to household "market income" (i.e., household income *before* taxes and transfers). The famous U-shaped trend emerges starkly in the classic results of Emmanuel Saez (see Figure 3).[4] We see inequality dropping precipitously in the late 1920s and during World War II, stabilizing at a comparatively low level over the next 30 years, and then taking off

Figure 3. Trends in the top decile income share

Note: The shares reported here pertain to market income (either including or excluding capital gains).

Source: Emmanuel Saez

in the 1970s and ultimately returning to the extreme levels that prevailed in the 1920s.

The foregoing results of course pertain to the top decile. What about the one percent that's so frequently featured in Occupy commentary? In Figure 4, it's shown that there's indeed good reason to feature the one percent in discussions of inequality, as they've been the main force driving the takeoff. The three trend lines in Figure 4 pertain to the top per-

Figure 4. Decomposing trends in the top decile income share

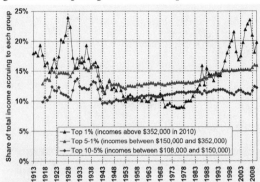

Note: The shares reported here pertain to market income (including capital gains).

Source: Emmanuel Saez

centile (i.e., household income exceeding $352,000 in 2010), the next 4 percent (i.e., household income between $150,000 and $352,000 in 2010), and the bottom half of the top decile (i.e., household income between $108,000 and $150,000 in 2010). The simple but dramatic conclusion emerging here is that the fluctuations of the top decile are mainly (but not entirely) due to fluctuations within the top percentile. That is, the shares of the lower-income groups haven't increased all that much in recent decades, whereas the share of the one percent has soared.

The foregoing results make it clear that, when the "golden years" of the 1940s, 1950s, and 1960s serve as a comparison point, there's no alternative but to characterize contemporary U.S. income inequality as extremely high. The share of national income going to the top percentile has roughly doubled during the half-century following those golden years. At the same time, the level of inequality that we're now experiencing is not entirely unprecedented, indeed both Figures 3 and 4 show that we've but returned to the extreme levels that prevailed in the late 1920s.

The trend in wealth inequality is perhaps more complicated. Because long-term trends are again of interest, the Survey of Consumer Finances (SCF) can't any longer be used (whereas Figure 2 was based on the SCF), and instead the best available source is IRS estate tax returns. The standard approach here, one that Wojciech Kopczuk and Emmanuel Saez have recently applied,[5] is to estimate the wealth holdings of the living population from estate tax returns by applying a multiplier that's based on the appropriate mortality rates. In Figure 5, we've presented the results from this approach, results that in fact contrast quite sharply with those presented for income inequality. Although wealth inequality, like income inequality, declined precipitously following the stock market crash of 1929, the trajectory thereafter is very

Figure 5. Trend in the wealth share of the top one percent

Note: The data are drawn from Wojciech Kopczuk and Emmanuel Saez, 2004, "Top Wealth Shares in the United States, 1916-2000: Evidence from Estate Tax Returns," National Tax Journal, Vol. LVII, No. 2, Part 2, June, pp. 445-87.

different from that for income inequality. The main difference: The share of income going to the top percent has taken off in the last 30 years (see Figure 4), whereas the share of wealth going to the top percent has been roughly stable during that same period. When the focus shifts to wealth inequality, one cannot tell a simple story of growing concentration among the one percent, a result that of course departs sharply from that for income inequality.

Although the one percent are not claiming an ever-rising share of national wealth, it's still possible to find evidence of growing wealth concentration within the more rarefied world of the Forbes 400 Wealthiest Americans. The latter group, which constitutes the top 0.0002%, has increased its share of national wealth from approximately 1.16 percent in 1983 to 3.15 percent in 2006 (see Figure 6). The available evidence further suggests that the mean net worth of this group has not declined very much in the recession and its aftermath.[6] It's only among the super-rich, then, that the data accord well with the popular view that

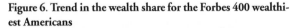

Figure 6. Trend in the wealth share for the Forbes 400 wealthiest Americans

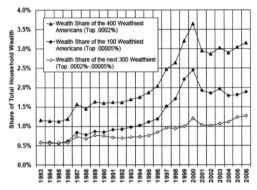

Note: The data are drawn from Wojciech Kopczuk and Emmanuel Saez, 2004, "Top Wealth Shares in the United States, 1916-2000: Evidence from Estate Tax Returns," National Tax Journal, Vol. LVII, No. 2, Part 2, June, pp. 445-87.

the richest individuals control an increasing share of the national wealth. This view has to be rejected for the far more inclusive top one percent.

Does this inconsistency between trends in income and wealth inequality among the one percent pose an intellectual puzzle? Not at all. We know that the dramatic growth in top income shares is mainly due to a growth in labor income rather than capital income.[7] The income of the one percent is rising, in other words, because the one percent is getting paid more for its labor, not because it is getting more returns from capital. What we don't know, however, is *why* the new high earners didn't become a true rentier class in the postwar period. Although there's no definitive evidence on this question, it's at least plausible that the steeply progressive income and estate taxes of the postwar period led to corresponding difficulties in accumulating wealth.[8] The implication of this line of reasoning is that, because taxes in the United States are now becoming less progressive, we might well see a new wave of wealth concentration and a new Gilded Age in the coming decades.

Cross-National Comparisons

The simple descriptive purpose of this chapter is to examine whether the conventional characterization of the United States as a high-inequality country is on the mark. To this point, we've shown that the well-known trends in income inequality are quite consistent with that conventional characterization, whereas the less-known trends in wealth inequality are more complicated and reveal a growing concentration only among the ranks of the super-rich. We now turn to the cross-national data and ask the analogous question: Does the United States stand out as an unusually unequal country when it's compared to other rich countries?

Because most countries have experienced substantial over-time change in their income distribution, the only way to carry out a satisfying cross-national comparison is to do so over a relatively long time period, a constraint that again makes the tax-return data the best source. Although a great many methodological complications arise when using tax statistics for the purpose of making cross-national comparisons, the key advantages of doing so are (a) the available time series cover an unusually long sweep of history, and (b) it becomes possible to measure the income shares of the top one percent and hence speak directly to the type of inequality that has so captivated the Occupy movement. We thus draw on the recent research of Anthony Atkinson, Thomas Piketty, and Emmanuel Saez that is based on carefully harmonized tax statistics from 22 countries.[9]

For purposes of brevity, we'll present the trends in income inequality for just two classes of countries, the English speaking countries (i.e., the U.S., Canada, Ireland, the U.K., Australia, and New Zealand), and the Central European countries (i.e., France, Netherlands, Germany, and Switzerland). We will also include Japan in the latter category because its trajectory is similar to that of the Central European cases. The income data for all of these countries, which we've presented in Figures 7 and 8, pertain to the income share of the top one percent after excluding realized capital gains.

The trend line for the English-speaking countries, all of which run so-called liberal economies, assumes much the same U-shaped form that we earlier reported for the U.S. case (see Figure 7). But a starkly different form emerges for the Central Eu-

Figure 7. Trend in the top one percent share for English-speaking countries

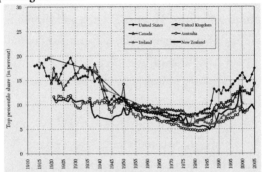

Figure 8. Trend in the top one percent share for Middle Europe and Japan

Note: The data presented here were drawn from Anthony B. Atkinson, Thomas Piketty, and Emmanuel Saez. 2011. "Top Incomes in the Long Run of History." Journal of Economic Literature 49:1, pp. 3-71.

ropean countries and Japan. As shown in Figure 8, these countries do undergo a real decline in inequality during the first half of the 20th century, but that decline is *not* followed by any subsequent rebound in inequality of the sort found in the U.S. and the other English-speaking countries. For the Central European countries (and Japan), one instead finds a rough stability in the amount of inequality or, in a few cases, even a continuing slight decline (i.e., the Netherlands especially and perhaps Switzerland).

The U.S. case thus stands out against that of other rich countries in at least two important respects. First, it's within that special class of countries experiencing a U-shaped trend, meaning that inequality has rebounded quite spectacularly in the latter part of the 20th century. This rebound did not happen everywhere (as Figure 8 reveals). Second, even within that class of countries that *did* experience the rebound, Figure 7 shows that the U.S. experienced it in especially virulent form. We started off in the early 20th century with especially extreme inequality and also ended up in the early 21st century with especially extreme inequality. It was only in the middle of the 20th century, when the U.S. had reached the bottom of its U-shaped curve, that it registered a quite average amount of inequality and appeared to be a generic rich country. This now appears to have been an unusual and misleading moment in U.S. history. Although there's a wide class of countries that have followed the U-shaped form, the U.S. has followed that form in an unusually extreme way.

The Sources of Inequality

We have to this point evaluated economic inequality in the U.S. against what has prevailed in the past and in other countries. As a final comparative exercise, we'll next consider whether present-day inequality exceeds what prevails in a competitive economy that rewards workers on the basis of their contribution to the economy (i.e., "marginal product"), a standard that has an almost mythic hold on U.S. judgments about inequality. The key question here is whether the extreme inequality in the United States may be understood as the price one pays for running a highly competitive economy in which individual contributions simply happen to be quite unequal.

This question matters because many Americans would find inequality less troubling insofar as they could be assured that it's simply a byproduct of our insistence on an efficient and competitive economy. In any standard opinion survey, a stock result is that many Americans are willing to tolerate substantial inequality provided that it's the outcome of an open, competitive, and fair contest and thus reflects the contributions that each individual has made to the economy (i.e., "marginal product"). If, however, there's a substantial disjuncture between contribution and income, then many Americans will call the resulting inequality into question. This issue can be addressed by examining how various institutions have the capacity to make income higher or lower than one's contribution to economic output.

The best-known institution by which such a disjuncture might be introduced is of course the U.S. government and its capacity to tax households and transfer income in ways that reduce inequality. Because average tax rates increase as income rises, and because transfers tend to boost income at the bottom of the distribution, the overall effect of taxes and transfers is to make incomes more equal. For some Americans (i.e., conservatives), the recent rise in inequality is less troubling to the extent that it's driven by a reduction in taxes and transfers, as such a reduction is valued for "ending handouts" and thereby bringing contributions and income into better alignment. For other Americans (i.e., liberals), the recent rise in inequality is *more* troubling if it's driven by a decline in taxes and transfers, as such a result means that the government is defaulting on its obligation to compensate for unequal opportunities and to provide a buffer against a harshly competitive market economy. In either case, the protagonists care deeply about whether the takeoff is attributable to changes in taxes and transfers, although those possible changes are evaluated very differently.

The best way to gauge the role of taxes and transfers in the takeoff is to revisit the Congressional Budget Office (CBO) estimates with which we led off.[10] The two key results from these estimates are that (a) taxes and transfers are not reducing inequality as much as they once did, and (b) the takeoff in income inequality is nonetheless mainly driven by forces other than the declining redistributive impact of government. The first result, with which we'll start, is especially critical. In its now-classic 2011 report, the CBO estimates that federal taxes and transfers reduced inequality by 23 percent in 1979, whereas they reduced inequality only by 17 percent in 2007. This decline arose because federal taxes shrank as a share of market income and because taxes and the distribution of transfers became less progressive. The simple consequence of these changes is that households at the bottom of the distribution are, on average, benefiting less from government tax and transfer policy than they did in the past. We can interpret this result as a partial realization of the conservative commitment to bring income into better alignment with the economic contributions that workers make.

The CBO report goes on, however, to establish that the declining redistributive effect of government cannot explain all that much of the recent takeoff in income inequality. The CBO graph reproduced in Figure 9 shows that the trend line for market inequality is only slightly less steep than the trend line for post-redistribution inequality. It follows that the debate between conservatives and Occupy supporters about the role of government in generating inequality has gone somewhat off track. This debate has focused obsessively on issues of redistribution even though the takeoff in inequality has little to do with changes in redistributive practices. If Occupy supporters can't legitimately blame much of rising inequality on tax rebates to the rich, nor can conservatives revel in the increase as tax-related and thus liberty-increasing. The takeoff is instead mainly

Figure 9. Trends in income inequality before and after transfers and taxes

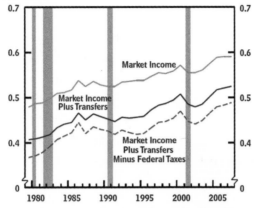

Note: These data are drawn from the Congressional Budget Office.

driven by various forces within the market that determine the distribution of income *before* taxes are assessed and transfers are made. The rest of this section will accordingly be devoted to a discussion of some of those labor market forces.

We begin by considering the role of unions in accounting for the takeoff in inequality. We do so because unions are conventionally understood as one of the main labor market institutions allowing workers to secure incomes in excess of what they would obtain in a narrowly competitive market. If government tax and transfer policy has arguably been the primary compensatory institution of this sort, then unions have historically been a secondary means of ensuring that workers needn't settle for incomes equaling the competitive wage. There are two main ways in which unions help workers. Most obviously, they raise the wages of union members by providing them with a monopoly over certain jobs, in effect preventing employers from driving down wages by pitting union and nonunion workers against one another. But equally important they also raise the wages of nonunion workers because (a) employers wish to forestall unionization (i.e., the threat effect), and (b) the union wage generates widely-shared norms about proper pay that are then costly for employers of nonunion workers to ignore (i.e., the moral economy effect).[11] Although unions have historically reduced inequality in both ways, we're interested in assessing whether such equalizing effects are waning with the historic decline in the proportion of workers who are unionized.[12]

In addressing this question, we're obliged to turn to the Current Population Survey (CPS), as it includes information on union membership and other relevant individual determinants of wages. We rely in particular on the recent research of Bruce Western and Jake Rosenfeld examining the effects of unions not just on the wages of union workers but also on the wages of nonunion workers who, as discussed above, indirectly benefit from the norms of fair pay promulgated by unions.[13] The core result of their research is presented in Figure 10. The top line in this figure pertains to the actual increase in wage inequality, and the bottom line pertains to the increase in wage inequality that would have obtained had unionization remained at the very high level (i.e., 34 percent) that prevailed in 1973.[14] The differing slopes of these two lines implies that approximately one third of the rise in inequality is attributable to the decline in unionization between 1973 to 2007.[15] It follows that the working class has

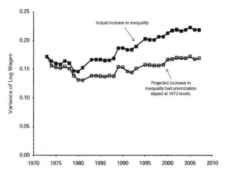

Note: The figure is drawn from Bruce Western and Jake Rosenfeld, 2011, "Unions, Norms, and the Rise in U.S. Wage Inequality," American Sociological Review 76, pp. 513-37. The income data pertain to the hourly wages of full-time private-sector male, and inequality is measured as the variance of log wages between groups defined by age, race, ethnicity, education, region, union membership, and region-industry unionization rates.

lost out not just because taxes and transfers benefit it less but also because unions no longer play an important role in driving up its wages.

These two results thus speak to the inequality-increasing effects of obliging the bottom of the class structure to make do with a narrowly competitive wage. For those who are troubled by inequality, it's

unfortunate that some of the institutional forces behind the takeoff have widespread popular support, a
support that's grounded in a moral commitment to a
competitive economy (or, more precisely, a commitment to the conventional accoutrements of a competitive economy). In the United States, we vilify transfer
programs as mere handouts, and we're suspicious of all
institutions, such as unions, that can be represented
as anti-competitive. It may accordingly be difficult
to roll back inequality by simply reestablishing the
institutional forms that once moderated it.

It's instructive to ask whether the main institutional developments at the top of the class structure
may likewise be understood as consistent with this
commitment to a competitive economy. This question has been addressed most prominently by scholars
attempting to account for the rising payout to CEOs.
The takeoff in CEO pay is itself incontrovertible: The
average compensation of CEOs, when divided by the
average compensation of production workers, yields
a ratio that increases from 24.2 in 1965 to 185.3 in

2009.[16] Although some scholars argue that weaknesses in corporate governance have allowed CEOs to pay themselves in excess of their contribution, others argue that rising compensation merely reflects weakening norms against interfirm CEO mobility as well as the increasingly consequential decisions of CEOs operating in a fast-moving global economy.[17] The former account suggests that the economy at the top of the class structure is becoming less competitive, whereas the latter suggests that it's becoming more competitive. We won't attempt to weigh in on this debate because it remains so unsettled at this point.

The analogous debate also emerges in research on the role of education in the takeoff in inequality. The facts themselves are again quite clear: It's well established that the rising payoff to college and post-college schooling is an importance source of the takeoff in earnings inequality.[18] It's less clear, however, *why* the payoff to schooling is increasing and in particular whether the increase is driven by (a) the rising demand for and productivity of college-educated workers (i.e., "skill-biased technological change"), or (b) a persistent shortage of workers that arises because children born into poor families don't have a full opportunity to attend college (i.e., the "bottleneck narrative").

The first of these two narratives emphasizes that technological change, especially the computerization of the workplace, serves to increase the demand for educated labor. Because this demand can't be immediately met, the payoff to educated labor increases as employers compete with one another and bid up its price, and the earnings gap between educated and uneducated labor accordingly widens. The second narrative, by contrast, emphasizes that the supply of potential college students is artificially lowered because children born into poor families and neighborhoods don't have the training that qualifies them for entry into college. This bottleneck means that those lucky enough to have a college education are protected from competition and reap excessive pay as a result. If all children, even those born into poor families, had fair and open access to higher education, these excessive returns would disappear under the force of competition.

The bottleneck narrative thus partly attributes the takeoff in inequality to an educational system that denies poor children a full opportunity to go to college. The inequality that results from such a bottleneck is especially vulnerable to public critique because it violates our commitment to the free flow of labor and to an open and competitive economy. Obversely, the main inequality-generating forces at the bottom of the class structure (e.g., deunionization) are less vulnerable to criticism, indeed they're often defended and supported as competition-enhancing. It's not implausible that the Occupy movement has increasingly focused on the bottleneck critique precisely because it resonates so well with core American values.

Conclusions

The purpose of this chapter has been to lay out the main facts of economic inequality with data of unimpeachable quality. It's been conventional, at least since the Occupy movement broke out, to characterize the U.S. case as one of "much inequality." We've sought to specify more formally the types of comparisons that are or are not consistent with that conventional characterization. We've asked whether it can be upheld when comparing present-day data to (a) what prevailed in the past, (b) what prevails in other countries, or (c) what prevails in some ideal-typical world.

The trend data reveal a more complicated story than casual followers of the inequality literature might have imagined. Although the share of income going to the top percent has of course taken off in the last 30 years, the share of wealth going to the top percent has, by contrast, been roughly stable during that same period. The latter result, which hasn't been widely publicized, appears to be one of the real triumphs of the comparatively aggressive tax policy of the postwar period. The high earners of the postwar period may have had difficulties accumulating wealth and becoming a true rentier class because income and estate taxes of that period were so steeply progressive.[19]

The cross-national data reveal a story that's more frequently rehearsed. When compared to other countries, the U.S. case stands out as starkly distinctive, indeed it's even extreme when the comparison is limited to other countries that have, like the U.S., experienced a U-shaped trend in inequality. The U.S. variant of that trend line is distinctive by virtue of its extreme inequality at both the beginning and end points. It was only in the middle of the 20th century, when the U.S. had reached the bottom of its U-shaped curve, that it registered a quite average amount of inequality and showed up as a generic rich country.

We concluded by asking how the U.S. measures up against various "institutional ideals" rather than existing societies. Although there are many such ideals in play (see "Ethics and Inequality"), we've focused on the competitive-market ideal because it's a touchstone for so many Americans. We've thus asked whether the main inequality-generating changes underway are bringing us closer or further to that ideal. The answer to this question would appear to vary by sector. At the bottom of the class structure, it's the standard story of various "anti-competitive" protections for workers, such as unions, facing an increasingly hostile reception and playing an ever-diminished role. At the top of the class structure, the analogous "anti-competitive" practices (e.g., rationing education, CEO overpay) are largely hidden from view, have not been delegitimated, and may well be generating much illicit inequality. It's precisely this double standard that at least some members of the Occupy movement have sought to target.

Ethics and Inequality

Rob Reich and Debra Satz

CONSIDER SOME FACTS: THE 400 WEALTHIEST Americans have more money than the bottom 50 percent of all Americans combined. Between 1979 and 2007, the incomes of the top one percent of the population grew by 275 percent while the incomes of the middle class rose less than 40 percent. According to newly released 2011 measures, a staggering one in three Americans, or 100 million people, suffer in poverty or near poverty.[1]

These are startling facts, and the Occupy Movement, with its references to the "1%" and the "99%," has successfully brought such inequalities to the fore of public consciousness. In response, some believe that such popular protest against inequality is inspired by mere envy, or an effort to inflame class warfare. We disagree. Inequalities can—in this case do—raise ethical concerns, and we think citizens are right to be outraged at the gap between the 1% and the 99%. We seek here to explain why these inequalities are so troubling.

But first, let us say the obvious: inequality in itself is not always wrong. Indeed, some inequalities are both inevitable and desirable. In a market economy, we expect inequalities of income. More generally, a world in which there were no differences between people is hard to imagine: we are unequal in so many ways. Some work harder, some are more talented, some are more comfortable with taking risks. American society has always recognized that there can be legitimate reasons for rewarding people unequally. Therefore, it is important to ask what forms of inequality are morally objectionable.

A great diversity of objections to inequality can be raised. We highlight four reasons to object to the kinds of inequalities mentioned above: they concern *opportunity, civic status, fairness, and the nation's welfare.* These reasons strike at the heart of American values and of the values of any liberal democracy.

The first reason to object to our gaping income and wealth differentials is that vast economic inequalities and concentrated wealth in the hands of the few are incompatible with affording everyone genuine opportunity and social mobility. We Americans celebrate the possibility that children from all walks of life have similar chances of success. The idea of equality of opportunity enjoys wide acceptance. It is the core of the American Dream. But when income gaps are very large and persist over time, the wealthiest possess systematic advantages over the poor: advantages in education, in health, in personal security. Social mobility in America is *lower today* than a generation ago. The accident of birth is highly predictive of one's life chances; people increasingly occupy fixed and frozen positions and pass these positions down to their children. In other words, children born into poor families tend to stay poor and children born into wealthy families generally stay rich. By contrast, intergenerational mobility today is greater in Canada, France, Germany, and the Scandinavian countries.[2]

Within the United States, a great deal of poverty is due to the institutional and social exclusion of the poor from a variety of settings: good schools, safe neighborhoods, quality day care, and health insurance. Astoundingly, about 30 million Americans have below basic literacy skills and cannot perform simple everyday literacy activities such as understanding newspaper articles; this statistic includes some non-immigrant Americans who cannot fill out a job application.[3] Students from advantaged family backgrounds are 25 times more likely to attend a top tier college than students from disadvantaged backgrounds.[4]

These deep intergenerational inequalities undermine the fairness of a system in which we expect people of roughly similar talent and motivation to have roughly similar chances of success independent of their social origins. Diversities in class, race and/

or gender never justify the automatic assignment of anyone to lesser social positions. But the growing inequalities that characterize American society today are at odds with equal opportunity. The result is a corrosion of meritocracy, the principle that mandates that economic positions and offices of influence are to be earned on the basis of merit. Instead, the processes we have now to distribute benefits and burdens to citizens shovel more and more to those born with silver spoons and offer fewer rewards for those with talent and who work hard.

The second reason to object to the growing income and wealth chasm is that vast economic inequalities create unequal citizenship. In democracies there can be no caste system; citizens must possess the same status. As a pre-existing status, citizenship does not depend on individual fortune, virtuous behavior, or even on contribution to society. But, as we have just seen, very large differentials in income translate into systematic advantages: in political influence, in access to jobs and positions of authority, in health, in personal security, in the opportunity to develop one's talents. When unequal wealth can systematically purchase advantage in each of these domains, it is difficult to face each other as social equals. As inequality has grown, the fate of the few has become unhinged from the fate of the many, as the wealthy find security in cloistered neighborhoods, send their children to private schools, and attend sporting events in luxury skyboxes. Divided from one another, our unequal lives no longer reflect the fact that society depends on the productive contributions of us all. We no longer stand in a relation of equality to each other as fellow citizens; instead, a small and wealthy minority dominate a larger and poorer majority.

We worry about the general effects of massive income and wealth differentials, but we want to call special attention to its effect on politics. In a democracy, equal citizenship is foundational: every citizen has a vote and only one vote. But when money is speech and corporations are persons, and when politicians depend on contributions for election, the "1%" speak with megaphones and the rest of us with a whisper. It is only when the "99%" assemble that a people's microphone is possible.

In 2011, the "millionaires club" claimed fewer than one percent of Americans but 47 percent of their elected representatives in Congress.[5] And the wealthy not only form a large number of our political leaders, they also have disproportionate influence on the selection of these leaders. The 2010 U.S. Supreme Court decision, *Citizens United v. Federal Election Commission*, lifted all previous restrictions on independent spending by corporations for political purposes. The consequences of this decision have unleashed a massive new flow of private dollars, funneled through so-called SuperPACS (political action committees) to support the campaigns of various candidates for office, amplifying the already unequal voice of the wealthy in our democratic system.

The unlimited influence of office and of wealth close off opportunities for everyone else. The rich increasingly buy office and power, control the market, usurp for themselves a lion's share of the fruits of our common efforts, and exert strong influence on our society's policies. This pattern of private capture—borne out over and over again in human history—is why we cannot have a genuine democracy where there are massive inequalities. The steep slope of privilege does not only hurt the poor: all of us are harmed when social justice is subordinated to private interest.

Third, the canyon between the "1%" and the "99%" is not the result of a fair process, where the rules and rulers of the game are equally responsive to the interests of all persons. Some inequalities are justified by the manner in which they came about. But the inequalities in life prospects of Americans today are the result of laws and institutions that cater to the very rich and have ceased to be responsive to the vast majority. Tax burdens on the wealthy have dropped to the lowest rate in many decades, and the changes in the tax code—specifically the decline in progressive tax rates and the significantly reduced estate tax—

have benefited the very wealthy far more than other taxpayers, exacerbating the already growing gap in pre-tax earnings. Average tax rates for the wealthiest 0.1 percent of Americans have trended downward for fifty years.[6] Apart from tax on individuals, loopholes abound so that corporations can post enormous profits but escape taxation altogether. Corporate lobbyists have massive influence on the rules of the game, while the wealthy disproportionately influence the political process and disproportionately win elected office. It is no surprise then that our tax policies and campaign-finance laws are not the result of, and do not reflect, the interests of most Americans.

Finally, new research suggests that the deep inequality which pervades American society today also threatens the economic welfare of the nation.[7] This is so for three possible reasons. First, if rising inequality tends to diminish genuine opportunity for all, then intergenerational mobility is threatened, eroding a dynamic social structure in which talent and hard work are rewarded. Second, massive income inequality can reduce demand and consumption in the economy. When the wealthiest capture larger and larger shares of income, the nation's wealth is concentrated ever more highly at the very top. But the wealthy have a greater marginal tendency than the middle class to save rather than spend their wealth, lowering aggregate demand in the economy. Third, some research shows that greater income equality is connected with long term and stable economic growth, as well as better worker morale and productivity. In sum, massive inequality such as we now see in the United States is a drag on the wealth of the nation. And an efficient, vibrant and growing economy is an ethical concern too. Economic decline invariably hits the poor the hardest.

What, then, has been the result of the unprecedented levels of inequality in American society? A society riven by lack of genuine opportunity, unequal civic status, systematic unfairness, and an inefficient and unhealthy economy. For us, defending equality, and objecting to the outrageous inequalities between the "1%" and the "99%," is based on the democratic imperative to create a community where every citizen has a fair chance at a decent life, an equal opportunity to develop their talents and an equal voice in political decisions. This aspiration for a "society of equals" finds its taproot not in envy or class resentment but in our country's founding ideals and the democratic dreams of peoples everywhere.

III

The Sources of the Takeoff

Increasing Income Inequality:
Economics and Institutional Ethics

Kenneth J. Arrow

THE SPECIFIC PROBLEMS OF THE CURRENT UNITED
States economy, the drastic increase in unemployment
and sluggish increase in output, overlay a tendency of
much longer duration, a drastic and rapid increase in
the inequality of income. Every economy of any com-
plexity has an unequal distribution of the good things
in life. But the period immediately following World
War II showed a considerably increased equality of income compared with either the Great Depression or the
previous period of relatively normal economic activity.

Since the middle 1980s, this tendency has been
reversed. In the United States, the median family in-

come has remained virtually constant since 1995. It has risen only 2 percent since 1985, while the mean family income rose at about 20 percent during the same period.[1] This obviously is possible only if incomes in the upper half of the income distribution are rising considerably more rapidly than those in the lower half. The difference in income between college graduates and those graduating only high school increased at a rapid rate during the period before 1990. More precisely, the income of college graduates remained roughly constant from 1975 to 1990, while the incomes of those completing only high school fell about 20 percent during the same period. Since 1990, the income of high school graduates has fallen slightly, while the income of college graduate students has remained roughly constant.[2] Hence, even college graduates have not participated in the economic growth of the country, while the condition of those of lower educational attainments have deteriorated considerably. While the proportion of the population over 25 that has a college degree has increased over time, it is still only about 30 percent, compared with 23 percent in 1995.[3]

Clearly, the bulk of increased productivity went to a small group of upper-income recipients. Even the average student who completed college did not gain anything, and those of lower educational level lost, both in absolute terms, without taking account of the general (if slow) increase in *per capita* income. Indeed, closer study showed that the bulk of the increase went to the top 1 percent of income recipients and much of that to those in the top 0.1 percent. The most detailed analysis is that of Piketty and Saez.[4] From 1913 through 1941, the share of income going to the top 1 percent of income recipients was never less than 15 precent. (Income here does not include capital gains.) The proportion then fell through World War II and thereafter, falling below 8 percent for most of the years 1970-1978. Then the proportion started rising rapidly, over 15 percent for all but two years during 1998-2008, rising to over 18 percent in 2007. A similar picture appears if one looks at the proportion of income going to the top 0.1 percent, which received nearly 8 percent of total income in 2008. There is some tendency in the data for the distribution within the top 1 percent to be more concentrated when the overall distribution is more concentrated.

The causes of this growing inequality are varied. There has been a steady attack on the use of the tax system as a means of equalizing income. The income and estate taxes have been the most directly effective in redistribution. The top rate in the Federal income tax was over 90 percent in the 1950s and is 35 percent today. The exemption level for estate taxes has risen steadily. In 2010 dollars, it was $426,000 in 1980, $1,000,100 in 1990, $855,000 in 2000, and $4,847,000 today.[5] On the other hand, the earned income tax credit has actually permitted negative income taxes (payments by the government to the tax filer) at the lowest end.

Beyond changes in the tax system, we have seen dramatic changes in the economy and structure of opportunity in the labor force. Shifts in the composition of goods and services have reduced income opportunities for many. Skilled industrial jobs have disappeared, while growing information services required a different set of skills. Employment in manufacturing reached over 19 million in 1979 and 1980 and has fallen to 14 million in 2007[6] (before the 2008 recession), despite a considerable increase in the labor force. This shift has undoubtedly been accelerated by globalization, with considerable imports of manufactured goods. The role of labor unions in promoting equality is not very clear, but in any case union membership in the private sector has declined sharply, from 24 percent in 1973 to 7 percent today.[7] The weakening of the unions is in good measure attributable to the relative decline in manufacturing, where unionization is easier.

Contemporaneous with the decline of manufacturing has been the increase of two service industries, finance and health. The finance industry should, in principle, receive its profits as a reward for improving the allocation of capital. These profits have, however, always been a significant fraction of total profits, not a small fee. The ratio of profits in the finance industry to total profits of domestic industry was below 20 percent until 1985, but have exceeded 30 percent since 1999.[8] Their labor needs are, of course, directed in considerable measure to the best-educated and are rewarded with very high incomes.

The notion of a well-running market is not too inappropriate for manufactured goods. The different items are produced to be alike and can be evaluated by consumers. But the products of the finance and health industries are individualized and complex. The consumer cannot seriously evaluate them, a situation that economists call "asymmetric information."

This casts a light on the claim that the problem is one of personal ethics, of, "greed." After all, the search for improvement in technology and consequently in the general standards of living is motivated by greed. When the market system works properly, greed is tempered by competition. Hence, most of the gains due to innovation and good service cannot be retained by the providers.

But in situations of asymmetric information, the forces of competition are weakened. The individual patient or client of a financial firm does not have access to all the relevant information. Indeed, when the information is sufficiently complex, it may not even be possible for anyone to provide adequate information.

In these circumstances, the concept of "greed" becomes more relevant. There arises an obligation to present the relevant information as fully as possible, an obligation which has been violated in the financial industry. In the medical field, this issue has to a considerable extent been met historically by standards of proper practice. These may involve revelation of all information or at least require that the differences of information not be exploited.

It is clear that the financial industry is well behind the medical in this respect. The sense of responsibility has to be enforced by legislation, as indeed was already the case in the 1930s. There has been some erosion in the law, under the Clinton administration, and some in the enforcement of the law. The Dodd-Frank law is a step in the right direction, but the influence of the financial industry watered it down and created unnecessary complications.

It is, of course, not superfluous to argue that a steepening of the income tax progression, removal of a number of blatant loopholes, including ending the special treatment of capital gains, and reduction of the exemption level for estates would add considerably to post-tax equality.

Why Is There So Much Poverty?

David B. Grusky and Kim A. Weeden

THE UNITED STATES, ONE OF THE RICHEST countries in the world, has a problem with poverty. There's just too much of it.

The latest statistics show that 49 million Americans are in poverty and another 90 million are in "near-poverty" (i.e., have incomes less than twice the poverty line).[1] These two groups, which together account for 48 percent of all Americans, would form a country with a population ranked the tenth largest in the world. Although many Americans assume that poverty is mainly found elsewhere, in fact the poverty in some parts of the United States is as dire and concentrated as it gets.

We have long been a high-poverty country. As shown in Figure 1, the official poverty measure dropped to a historic low of 11.1 percent in 1973, but that level was never again achieved over the course of the following four decades. The recent recession, like most prior ones, has caused a surge in poverty. The official poverty measure now stands at 15.0 per-

Figure 1. Trends in the size of the official poverty population and in the official poverty rate

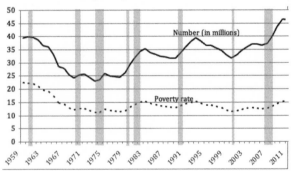

Note: Data are from the Current Population Survey (2012). Shaded bars indicate recessions.

cent, the highest level in the last half century, and most scholars expect that poverty will remain high for many more years.

Why are high poverty rates such an entrenched feature of U.S. life? The standard argument here is that our high poverty rate is an unfortunate byproduct of running a competitive and deregulated economy. If we really want less poverty, so the argument goes, we have no choice but to opt for European-style market regulations that have the unfortunate side effect of strangling productivity and reducing output. The standard-issue economist thus intones that Europeans pay dearly for their comparatively low poverty rate by settling for a much reduced gross national product (GNP). Under the American formula, by contrast, we opt for a highly competitive and regulation-free economy, with the happy result that there are more goods and services for everyone. To be sure, the cost of this choice is a high poverty rate, but in principle we could choose to spend some part of our large national product on a better safety net for the poor.

The foregoing story, however frequently repeated, is wildly off the mark. What's wrong with it? The first point that should be made is that, even though we could choose to use our relatively large GNP to build a strong safety net, we haven't opted to do so. As is well known, the United States has a distinctively anemic safety net: We rank a stunning 29th among the 32 richest countries in the amount of income support provided to those who have lost their jobs (see Figure 2). Because

Figure 2. Percentage of net income replacement in the first five years after job loss [i.e., (net benefits)/(net earnings when employed) x 100]

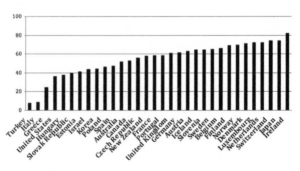

Source: OECD, Benefits and Wages 2010. Paris: OECD, 2012.

our safety net is so underdeveloped, some commentators have suggested that the best way to take on U.S. poverty is to build a better safety net, a prescription that takes for granted the high rates of poverty generated by our economy and accordingly focuses our reform efforts on after-market remediation.

We should indeed build a better safety net. But we shouldn't also rule out reforming the labor market institutions that are overwhelming our safety net with so much poverty in the first place. The main reason why labor market reforms tend not to be on the table is, as we've noted, the widely-shared presumption that the U.S. economy is finely-tuned for competition and efficiency. The obvious corollary of this presumption is that any tinkering with the labor market (e.g., increasing the minimum wage) would introduce inefficiencies, reduce total output, and thus make it even more difficult to afford an enlarged safety net.

This brings us to our second point that our market institutions, far from being efficient, are instead riddled with bottlenecks that are both inefficient

Figure 3. Average monthly unemployment rate of civilian population, age 25 or older

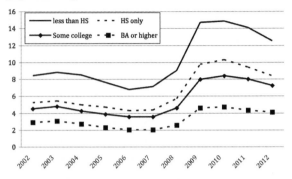

Source: Current Population Survey (Bureau of Labor Statistics, 2012).

and poverty-generating. The real reason, in other words, why we have so much poverty is that we're running an uncompetitive economy that protects the rich from competition and prevents the poor from competing.

This is a strong claim but we can offer some support for it. The high unemployment and low wages among poorly-educated workers arises in part because there are just too many of them chasing after the few jobs for which they're qualified. In effect, there's a vast reserve army of poorly educated labor, with the result that unemployment among such labor is extremely high and wages extremely low. As shown in Figure 3, about thirteen percent of the least-educated workers are now unemployed, whereas only four percent of those who are college-educated are unemployed. The returns to a college education are also increasing and imply an ever-worsening market situation for the less-educated (see Figure 4). Although recent college graduates can't always find good jobs, the scholars trumpeting the travails of the college educated haven't appreciated that the recession has hit less-educated workers yet harder;[2] and hence the advantage of college graduates relative to the less-educated remains substantial and is growing.

The latter results are suggestive of uncompetitive practices. If our economy were truly competitive, labor would freely flow to where returns are highest, and growing cross-sector disparities in earnings would induce workers to secure the requisite education. This hasn't happened.

Figure 4. Trends in the wage benefits to completing college relative to high school

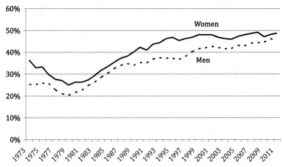

Source: State of Working America, 12th Edition *(Economic Policy Institute, 2012). Estimates are adjusted for race, ethnicity, age as a quartic, marital status, and region, and indicate the percentage by which the hourly wages of a college graduate (BA only) exceed those of a high school graduate with no college, all else equal.*

Why haven't the ranks of the reserve army been thinned out as less-educated workers react to their increasingly difficult labor market situation? Although there are many reasons for this puzzling behavior, an especially important one is that two types of bottlenecks are preventing workers from behaving as they would in a truly competitive market. The supply of potential college students is artificially lowered because children born into disadvantaged families are poorly prepared for college and, in any event, lack the money to afford it. The supply of college graduates is also kept artificially low because the best private universities ration their available slots and the best public universities haven't any funds to expand. Is Stanford University, for example, meeting the rising interest in its degrees by selling some profit-maximizing number of them? Have top public institutions stepped into the breach and increased the number of available slots? The evidence indicates very clearly that they haven't.

This is not how a competitive market works. When the demand for hybrid cars, for example, increased dramatically in the U.S., car manufacturers didn't set up "admissions committees" charged with evaluating the qualifications of prospective buyers. Instead, they ramped up production to a profit-maximizing level, and the shortage-driven uptick in prices soon corrected itself. There's no such self-correcting feature built into our education system.

To the contrary, college degrees are carefully meted out, and the returns to a college degree have accordingly remained artificially high. We have become so accommodated to the high prices for college-educated labor that we don't appreciate the rationing that underlies them.[3]

This failure in the education market generates failure in the labor market by bloating the ranks of the poorly-educated class. If overcrowding at the bottom of the labor market were eased by making education more widely available, the market situation of workers would improve because (a) those who secured college degrees would earn more as a result, and (b) those who didn't take advantage of their newfound educational opportunities would still benefit because some of their former competitors have now been siphoned off. The best way to raise wages for the working poor is to trim the size of the reserve army and thereby limit the number of competitors chasing after the shrinking supply of low-skill jobs.

The two main alternatives to labor market reform are (a) protectionist policies designed to increase the number of manufacturing jobs in the U.S., and (b) a ramped-up safety net that delivers more benefits to unemployed or poor workers. The main disadvantage of both approaches is that they don't resonate well with our core commitments to a competitive and pro-work economy. Because of these commitments, many in the U.S. are deeply suspicious of protectionist policies, and most are opposed to a European-style safety net that provides substantial benefits to those who aren't working for pay. The simple implication: By addressing poverty with protectionism or redistribution, we could indeed prop up the bottom of the distribution, but with all the angst and opposition that such policies evoke in a pro-market society. In times of crisis, protectionist or Europeanist policies may sometimes be muscled through, but support for them will ultimately weaken as the economy rebounds, cries for "less regulation" intensify, and our core values reassert themselves. This dynamic was revealed, for example, in the widespread opposition to the most recent stimulus package (i.e., the American Recovery and Reinvestment Act of 2009) despite ample evidence that it successfully reduced poverty.[4]

Does this mean that we're consigned to running a high-poverty regime in the United States? Not at all. We've argued here that there's a third road available that allows us to fight poverty successfully within the context of our core commitments. It's hardly un-American to suggest that all children, rich and poor alike, should be provided a high-quality primary and secondary education that allows them to go to college and to pursue the high returns that college affords.

If the reform that we're advocating is straight-forwardly consistent with our core values and commitments, it's nonetheless radical in the sense that it requires taking those commitments seriously. It will not suffice to continue on with the usual half-hearted reform efforts. We need a radical overhaul of our education system to provide the same opportunities to all children and to provide enough higher-education slots to meet the additional demand that equalizing reform would generate.

In the education reform industry, most initiatives are promoted on the basis of their effects on "school quality," and any effects on equalizing opportunity are treated as a convenient side benefit. That is a betrayal of our core values. We should instead make the issue of equalizing opportunity central to all discussions of educational policy. This should be our main goal in just the same way that equalizing civil rights was in the 1960s and 1970s.

If we were to commit to this objective, as many other countries have, we could readily choose from a wide range of reforms in implementing it. We could choose to allocate opportunities via lottery rather than money (as South Korea has); we could choose to equalize early childhood training; we could choose to equalize the quality of primary and secondary training; or we could choose to commit seriously to eliminating financial barriers to access. This is not the place to debate which of these reforms is optimizing. There are many ways to skin the cat, and what matters for our argument is only that the cat be skinned. The main problem is not that we don't know how to secure equal opportunity. We've just given up on it and opted instead for a lip-service commitment to one of the core values of our country.

The Occupy narrative, which has recently emphasized just such issues of educational access, is quite consistent with the logic of institutional reform laid out here. It has been disheartening to watch commentators, even sympathetic ones, try to shoehorn the Occupy protests into some radical anti-American agenda. If there's anything at all radical about those protests, it's simply that core American values of fair competition and equal opportunity have finally been taken seriously.

IV

*Who Bears the Brunt
of the Takeoff?*

Education and Inequality

Sean F. Reardon

EDUCATION HAS LONG BEEN THE PRIMARY pathway to social mobility in the United States. The American Dream—the idea that one's family origin is no barrier to economic success—is plausible to the extent that we believe that our schools provide all students with equal opportunity to develop skills that will enable them to succeed in our complex society. Without such opportunity, hope for social mobility dims.

So when we ask whether America is becoming more or less equal, we should ask not only whether income and political power are becoming more unequally distributed,[1] but also whether social mobility is declining. We must ask whether children from all backgrounds have equal opportunities to develop to their full potential.

Increasingly, the answer seems to be no.

It is well known that economic inequality has been growing in the U.S. since the 1970s. Less well known, however, is the fact that inequality in educational success has also been growing. The difference in average academic achievement between high and low-income students is now 40 percent larger than it was 30 years ago. Indeed, the difference in average test scores between high- and low-income students is now much larger than the difference between black and white students.[2] This is evident in Figure 1, which shows trends in both the black-white reading test score gap and the test score gap between children in families with incomes at the 90th and 10th percentile of the family income distribution.

Likewise, the college completion rate for children from high-income families has grown sharply in the

Figure 1.

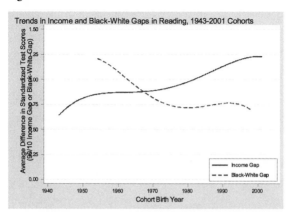

Trends in Income and Black-White Gaps in Reading, 1943-2001 Cohorts

Source: Reardon, 2011.

last few decades, while the completion rate for students from low-income families has barely moved. Moreover, high-income students make up an increasing share of the enrollment at the most selective colleges and universities. Not only are high-income children increasingly more likely to go to college, but they are more likely to go to a selective college. These trends are not due to the fact that higher-income students tend to have better educational opportunities in elementary and secondary schools and better test scores and academic records; even when comparing high- and low-income students with similar academic records, the same trends are evident.[3]

This rising gap in academic skills and college completion has come at a time when the economy relies more than ever on well-educated workers. Largely gone are the manufacturing jobs that provided a middle-class wage but did not require a college degree. In today's economy, young men and women without college degrees are often consigned to low-wage jobs with little opportunity for advancement. So family background has become increasingly determinative of educational success, and educational success, in turn, has become increasingly determinative of economic success.[4] Economic and social mobility—the extent to which children move to a different rung of the economic ladder from where they were born—has declined in the last 30 years.[5] As a result, the American dream has moved farther out of reach for lower-income children.

What has caused this rise in educational inequality? Contrary to popular rhetoric, test scores are not going down; our schools are not worse than they used to be. Indeed, the average nine-year-old today has math skills equivalent to those of the average eleven-year-old 30 years ago. Although reading skills and the math skills of high school students have not increased as much as the math scores of elementary and middle-school students, there is no evidence in national data of declining American students' math and reading skills.

Nor have test scores or college completion rates for students from low-income families declined; they simply haven't risen nearly as fast as those of high-income students. Although there are striking inequalities in the quality of schools available to children from low- and high-income families, these inequalities do not appear larger than in the past. Furthermore, if schools were responsible for widening educational inequality, we would expect that test-score gap to widen as students progress through school. But this does not happen. The test-score gap between eighth-grade students from high- and low-income families is no larger than the school-readiness gap among kindergarteners.[6] The roots of widening educational inequality appear to lie in early childhood, not in schools.

So what has been happening in early childhood? One troubling trend over the last four decades has been the significant increase neighborhood segregation by income (See Figure 2). In 1970, two-thirds of U.S. families lived in mixed-income, middle class

Figure 2.

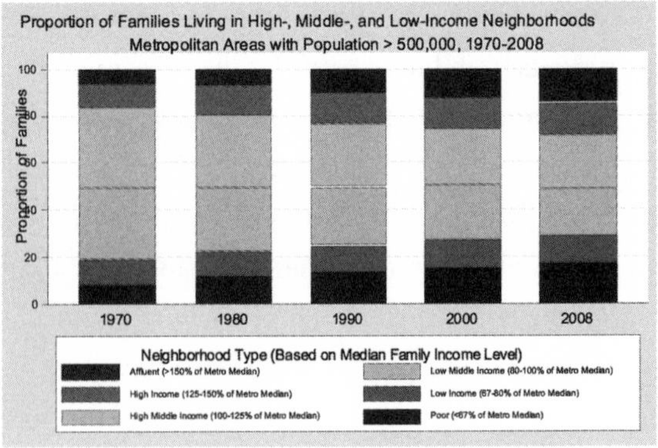

Proportion of Families Living in High-, Middle-, and Low-Income Neighborhoods
Metropolitan Areas with Population > 500,000, 1970-2008

Source: Reardon and Bischoff, 2011a, and author's calculations.

neighborhoods; Today, only 43 percent live in such neighborhoods, and one-third of all families now live in either very poor or very affluent neighborhoods. As a result, low-income children are increasingly likely to grow up in neighborhoods with few middle-class or affluent neighbors (and vice versa).[7] The absence of middle-class neighbors leads to fewer neighborhood resources, such as high-quality child care and pre-school opportunities. High-income families, by contrast, increasingly live in predominantly well-resourced, affluent neighborhoods where their children have access to numerous opportunities for healthy development.

In addition, high-income families increasingly invest more of their time and income in their children.[8] They spend more on preschool and early childhood education than they used to, more on tutors and lessons, on private school tuition, and on college. This is a rational response to an economy where educational success is increasingly important in securing a middle-class job. The problem, of course, is that lower-income families have not seen their income grow at the same rate as have upper-income families, and so they have not been able to increase their investment in their children. Stagnant incomes have left the poor and working-class without the resources to give their children the improved educational opportunities and supports that the children of the rich enjoy.

What can we do about this problem? The most effective way to narrow the academic achievement gap would be to ensure that all children have access to secure, stable, and cognitively stimulating environments in early childhood, both at home and in child-care or preschool settings. Family support programs, like the Nurse-Family Partnership, high-quality child-care services, and high-quality preschool programs for low- and middle-income children all have been shown to significantly improve the educational and behavioral outcomes of children. Many prominent scholars, including Nobel Laureate James Heckman, have demonstrated that investments in early childhood have long-term payoffs, both for the children directly affected by such investments and for society more broadly.[9]

In addition to investing in early childhood and schooling opportunities for disadvantaged youth, one of the best ways to ensure that all children have the opportunities to develop is to ensure that we have an economy that provides families with stable incomes at a living wage. Parents—all parents—are more effective at helping their children develop to their full potential when the parents have stable jobs and adequate health care. It is unlikely that meaningful reductions in educational inequality can be achieved without simultaneous efforts to reduce economic inequality.

These do not sound like education policies, perhaps, but the best way to reduce inequality in educational outcomes is to ensure that all students start school on a more even footing. Schools alone are unlikely to remedy the very large disparities among children entering the kindergarten door. We can—and must—do more to improve our schools, of course—particularly those schools that enroll low-income students. But schools alone cannot save the American Dream.

*The Double Binds of Economic
and Racial Inequality*

Prudence L. Carter

IN PRINCIPLE, THE UNITED STATES BECAME AN
"open society" in the mid-twentieth century upon
legally acknowledging the human and civil rights of
all of its citizens, including African, Asian, Latino,
Native, and other non-white Americans. In the wake
of democratic transformation and the expansion of
the opportunity to peoples of color of all socioeconomic statuses, a new debate emerged. Scholars and
policy makers began to ask if there were a declining
significance in race. The burgeoning rise of the African American middle class since the passage of the
Civil Rights Acts and the implementation of vari-

ous affirmative action practices created new classes of "haves" and "have nots." Further, the reality of higher median household incomes of some Asian ethnic groups than non-Hispanic Whites (U.S. Census 2012) and the election of the nation's first black president compel some to raise the question again: which has more significance in terms of inequality—class or race?

The Occupy movement has rightly focused our attention on the gross economic inequality that increased precipitously in the United States since the 1980s; those statistics are well-documented throughout this book. Still, while economic inequality affects our life chances and well-being, American society cannot afford to ignore the relationship between race and membership among the richest 1 percent, *as well as among* the middle and upper class strata of the 99 percent. Black, Latino, and Native American citizens are still more likely to be confronted with what it means to be at the bottom. The challenging questions must be asked: are we, the 99 percent, willing

Figure 1. Median Wealth Holdings by Race 1984-2007

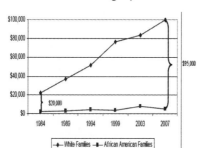

Source: Institute on Assets and Social Policy, Brandeis University

to see how we, too, collude in both racial and class inequality in the choices we make about whom we hire, where we live, where we send our children to school, where we worship, and how we create social networks? Despite the wide chasm between the rich and the non-rich, inextricable links between class *and* racial inequality endure, too, among the middle classes and the poor.

History speaks for itself about whether such universal class-based policies alone are sufficient to staunch inequality for all. Based on past experiences, we know that economic policies intended for the reduction of inequality have not affected people of color fairly and proportionately. Consider the following facts. The American middle class expanded after World War II and subsequent to the establishment of the Federal Housing Authority in 1934. Generous entitlements proffered by the GI Bill, including access to higher education, helped. But these government programs were not race neutral in their effects.[1] University segregation prevented many blacks and Latino GIs from obtaining higher education.[2] Racism also encouraged neighborhood redlining and thus limited black and Latino access to mortgage loans, as they sought the American dream through homeownership. In short, when the United States Congress designed policies and programs to decrease economic inequality and poverty and to build up the American middle class, those practices were not immune to certain forms of racial discrimination and exclusion.

During the latter half of the twentieth century, African Americans and Latinos did eventually gain greater access to home ownership—though often through predatory home loans that inflated the housing bubble. That housing success did not last long. After the 2008 recession hit, aggregate wealth plummeted in communities of color as the values of their homes depreciated, and thousands of families lost their houses to foreclosures. Discriminatory mortgage practices have caused a setback; and the opportunity to build assets through home ownership has vanished for many African American and Latino families who were already behind in terms of wealth accumulation.

Racially-coded predatory mortgage practices have compounded the wealth gap. Today, high earning, professional African Americans do not possess as much as lower-earning whites. In 2007, the average *middle*-income white household had $74,000 in wealth, whereas the average *upper*-income African American household had only $18,000.[3] Moreover, as Figure 1 shows, the wealth gap (not including home equity) between all African Americans and whites across all socioeconomic classes has quadrupled over a twenty-year period. And as of 2009, the median wealth of white households was twenty times that of black households and eighteen times that of Latino households (See Figure 2).[4]

In addition, the economic downturn has drastically reduced opportunities for employment. As Figure 3 shows, black unemployment is twice that of whites, a gap that occurred even in an economic growth period. The recession changed the situation

Figure 2.

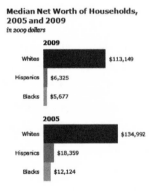

Median Net Worth of Households, 2005 and 2009
in 2009 dollars

2009
Whites — $113,149
Hispanics — $6,325
Blacks — $5,677

2005
Whites — $134,992
Hispanics — $18,359
Blacks — $12,124

Source: Pew Research Center tabulations of Survey of Income and Program Participation data

Figure 3. Unemployment rates, by race, and Hispanic or Latino ethnicity, 1975–2010

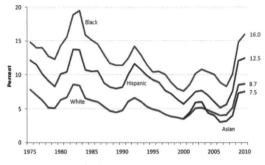

Source: U.S. Bureau of Labor Statistics

from bad to worse. While Latinos are better off than blacks, their unemployment rate is at least five percentage points higher than the corresponding rate for whites.[5] Some of the employment gap may owe to differences in education and skill levels, but even middle-class people of color with skills and education have taken a hit. In the civil rights era, when the United States opened up to the notion of racial equality in economic opportunity, many blacks sought civil service jobs in local, state, and national government. They are now experiencing another economic shock as layoffs and government-office closures mount. As the public sector sheds jobs, African American workers are hit the hardest. More than 25 percent of U.S. Postal Service employees, for example, are black, and a critical percentage has been laid off.[6]

The problem is not just about jobs and wealth. We find the same racial disparities in education. Many black and brown children attend schools that do not prepare them adequately.[7] A disproportionate share of our nation's urban schools continues to lag behind their wealthier, white suburban counterparts in resources and performance. And the dropout rate for Latinos is more than double the national average. The average white thirteen-year-old reads at a higher level and fares better in math than the average black or Latino seventeen-year-old.[8]

Differences in family resources among blacks, Latinos, and whites account for some of this, but it is not the sole explanation. Although the test-score disparity by race has narrowed over the last forty years, a significant differential still persists (see Reardon in this volume). And even when we compare the test scores—arguably, a very narrow measure of "educational success"—of black children from either affluent or middle class families to those of white children from equally affluent ones, black children's scores still lag behind.[9] Some of this difference is attributable to the fact that the resources and quality of schools attended by the typical black and Latino child—poor or middle class—are not equivalent to that of the typical poor or middle class white child.[10] Yet, even in resourceful and so-called high-quality schools, African American and Latino students have disparate educational experiences from their white peers. Researchers, many who have gone deeply within the folds of schools into classrooms and other educational spaces, have documented consistently the impact of racial disproportion in access to certain classes and content, as well as differential teacher expectations, evaluation, and treatment of children by race.[11]

Racial and class disparities in education also exacerbate other social and economic problems. At present, far too many of our African American and Latino youth are filling the juvenile justice and prison pipelines, which continue to expand. African American youth constitute 45 percent of juvenile arrests, although they comprise only 16 percent of the overall youth population. Their criminalization, particularly acute among males, begins early in school: K–12 black students are twice as likely as their white peers to be suspended and three times as likely to be expelled from school.[12]

To fundamentally attack economic inequality, the Occupy Movement cannot disregard how our society's economic and educational disparities are highly correlated with skin color and ethnicity. Some may view the injection of race matters into the discussion of economic inequality as resorting to limited identity politics. Or with President Obama in the White House, many Americans may want to believe that race no longer matters. To take that approach means to succumb to historical amnesia, however. Vast amounts of empirical data document how racism and racial discrimination—both past and present—intensify economic problems for people of color.[13] Economic inequality in the United States is not only a source but also a product of accumulated and continuing racial disadvantages. By being "colormute,"[14] or to avoid dealing with racial matters directly, the Occupy movement could run the risk of dangerous denialism, which will very well feed and fatten the beast it aims to annihilate.

Gender and Economic Inequality

Shelley J. Correll

AMONG THE TOP ONE PERCENT OF WAGE-EARNING Americans, women comprise a mere 12 percent.[1] On the 2011 Forbes list of the 100 richest people in America, only eight are women.[2] The Occupy movement has successfully drawn public attention to gross levels of economic inequality, and the policies that have created these inequalities, but has given less attention to inequalities within the top one percent—including a near-total dearth of women. Perhaps we see the lack of wealthy women as normal, natural, or even inevitable. Yet the allocation of economic resources in a society is anything but inevitable. Laws, public policies, workplace practices, and other social conventions and creations determine how wealth is parceled out, and who gets to hold on to how much of it.

Cultural ideas about gender permeate our policies and practices, constructing a system that rewards the activities men tend to perform, while ignoring or penalizing those more common to women. Consider, for example, tax policy. Tax codes are social creations that reward certain activities by taxing them at comparatively lower rates. In the U.S., capital gains income—a type of income more common among men—is taxed at a lower rate than other kinds of income. Indeed, capital gains are currently taxed at the lowest rate they have been in the past 60 years.[3] Some economists have argued that low capital gains taxes encourage people to invest in the stock market, which is good for the economy. But consider another type of behavior strengthening our economy's bottom line that our government *doesn't* recognize: the development of human capital.

According to the World Bank, social and human capital—that is, a nation's workforce—embodies as much as 59 percent of developed countries' wealth.[4] The development of that workforce happens primarily through unpaid carework, a task performed mostly by women,[5] and one that is economically penalized by U.S. policies.

For one, caregivers earn no direct social security credits for their contributions. An unmarried full-time caregiver who is not in the paid labor force (for example, a stay-at-home mom who lives with her partner but is unmarried, or a grandmother taking care of her grandchild) earns zero social security credits. If, however, the same person is married to a full-time paid worker, the couple earns 1.5 times the amount of credits that the full-time worker would have earned alone. In other words, an unpaid caregiver *only* gets credits when married to a paid worker—and even then, earns only half the amount the paid worker receives. Since women do twice as much carework as men, they suffer more of these penalties. (Interestingly, if a nanny provides carework for a baby, she earns social security credits, but a mother providing care to the same child does not.) And of course, mothers' caretaking also tends to free their partners to work more hours—indirectly benefitting workplaces. As journalist Ann Crittenden points out, this means that Americans "free ride" on the unpaid labor of mothers.

Although mothers (and a small number of fathers) cultivate human capital by serving as the primary caregiver for their children, this is not counted as "work" when calculating the Gross Domestic Product, because it is unpaid. Following the recommendation of the United Nations Statistical Association, Australia, Canada, Norway, France, Israel, and several other countries began collecting data on nonmarket work, including unpaid carework, as early as the 1990s.[6] So far, the U.S. has refused to do the same, claiming that it is difficult to pin a monetary value on caretaking. But estimates of the market value of unpaid non-market carework in the U.S., based on the amount of time spent performing it, suggest that its value is between 30 percent and 50 percent of the conventionally measured GDP.[7] This is simply too substantial of a contribution to go uncounted as "productive" work. Including unpaid carework in the GDP and offering social security credits for performing it would promote gender equality, acknowledge caretaking's importance, and inform policies that would not penalize the citizens who make this invaluable contribution to our nation's human capital.

Like public policies, workplace practices may also embody gendered ideas. One example of this is "overwork," which is defined as working more than 50 hours per week in the paid labor force. As sociologist Youngjoo Cha has shown, this work habit is disproportionately compensated: in 2008, those who overworked earned more per hour than those who did not. Men are the primary beneficiaries of this overcompensation, since overwork is more than twice as prevalent among professional men (36 percent) as among professional women (15 percent).[8] But the phenomenon of overcompensation for overwork (and the disproportionate benefit to men that results from it) is not inevitable; indeed, it is not even particularly longstanding. In 1979, the average hourly wage for overworkers was about 20 percent *less* than that of those who worked standard hours. It wasn't until more than two decades later that this trend reversed. In 1996, employers began paying overworkers more per hour than non-overworkers, and this trend continues to the present.[9]

Is there a logical rationale for this disproportionate compensation? Are those who work exceptionally long hours more "productive," and thus more deserving? Actually, psychological research suggests the opposite. Mental reasoning, problem solving, and decision-making are all hampered when cognitive resources are depleted.[10] As we repeatedly make the kinds of decisions that many professionals do at work, our resources are depleted and subsequent decisions become lower in quality. Depletion of cognitive resources also hampers task performance and increases procrastination.[11] After a certain amount of time at work, people simply cannot perform at their optimal capacity. In fact, those who overwork admit making more mistakes at work, and they express more frustration with their co-workers.[12]

Professor Leslie Perlow conducted a fascinating study that speaks directly to whether overwork translates into higher productivity or better workplace outcomes. In Perlow's experiment, some consulting teams at a large firm were assigned to a new schedule that required each team member to take one weekday off each week, with no contact to work, including email and voicemail. Consultants are known for working exceptionally long hours, a characteristic often considered fundamental to their job, so they can "always be available" for clients. What Perlow found was surprising. Rather than reducing the consultants' productivity, the reduction in work hours actually *enhanced* it. Once teams were required to take a day off, not only did their communication improve, but they also delivered a superior product to their clients.

The new schedule was so successful that the firm is expanding its implementation to more of its teams.

As these examples show, rewarding overwork defies economic rationality. The disproportionately high compensation for overwork appears to be expressive rather than functional, tacitly endorsing a single-minded commitment to paid work. As legal scholar Joan Williams has written, extra-long hours can only be worked by employees without competing responsibilities. More often than not, these workers are men. Men are much more likely than women to have a spouse who handles childcare and household work. Youngjoo Cha found that half of men who overwork have a wife who is unemployed or works part time. The same figure is only 13 percent for women.[13]

Just as workplaces reward activities more common among men, they punish activities more common among women. Consider family-related leave. Regardless of their sex, employees who take family leave earn lower salaries and are less likely to be promoted than those who do not.[14] At first glance, this seems reasonable, since taking a leave of absence means taking time away from work. But if this were true, we would expect employees who take leaves for non-family reasons to be equally penalized. However, this appears not to be the case. One study of university faculty found that those who take *family*-related leaves—more common among women—suffer a greater financial blow than those who take other types of leaves.[15]

Fundamentally, tax codes, social security laws, and workplace practices are statements about how we believe wealth should be apportioned, and what kind of services to society we value. These policies are highly malleable, not "natural" or inevitable; they have been changed countless times in the past, and could certainly be changed in the future. But by rewarding the activities usually performed by men and penalizing the ones usually performed by women, we widen the gender gap—effectively *manufacturing* gender-based economic inequality—by allowing cultural ideas about gender to infuse our public policies and workplace practices.

As a group, women are obviously harmed by policies that lead to economic gender disparities—but devaluing carework harms large numbers of men, too. Middle class and working class men are increasingly part of dual earner couples, contributing to household caregiving responsibilities and increasingly taking on more unpaid carework.[16] As a result, many men simply cannot be single-mindedly devoted to paid work. As is true for other policies, our country's treatment of carework disproportionately affects the non-wealthy, both women and men.

As the Occupy movement has successfully highlighted, our workplace practices and social policies are human creations that comprise hundreds of small decisions about what we value. But in thinking about how these policies could be restructured, it is crucial that the Occupy movement be mindful not just of the class divide, but of the large gender divide within social classes. If we ever want to have a fair system of wealth distribution, we're going to have to take into account existing gender inequalities. Allowing gender-based ideas and assumptions to infuse our definition of "productive" work harms society in multitudinous ways. Not only does it widen the economic gap between men and women, but it also creates penalties for caretaking—for contributing to the creation of healthy families and for raising the nation's future workforce. To reduce these kinds of inequalities, we need to pay greater attention to the ways that gender-based ideas and assumptions infuse the policies and practices that determine which activities we reward.

SHELLEY J. CORRELL   121

V

*Inequality, Politics,
and Democracy*

Restarting History

Gary Segura

THE COLLAPSE OF THE SOVIET BLOC IN THE LATE 1980s was, at the time, said to represent the ultimate triumph of liberal democracy and market capitalism as a social and economic system.[1] The free and open marketplace was the model for economic life as well as political life, and whatever defects or excesses in the model arose would be self-correcting. Marxist theorists and their misguided followers seriously underestimated the ability of capitalism (when married to democratic political structures) to reform itself, to impose enforceable checks on its worst excesses. As Francis Fukuyama (1989) solemnly declared, "The triumph of the West, of the Western idea, is evident first of all in the total exhaustion of viable systematic alternatives to Western liberalism."[2]

But consider the following:

In the fall of 2011, UC-Davis campus police officers casually pepper-sprayed defenseless students, seated peacefully on the ground, their "crime" being nothing more than refusing to leave the quadrangle. Like at Davis, police at UC-Berkeley, in Manhattan, and in locations across the country routinely used violence against non-violent OWS demonstrators. Elected officials and university administrators felt no compunction about using force to prevent the political dissent of these citizens and, in many instances, to keep these events obscured from the eyes and cameras of the press.

Contrast the treatment of OWS protestors by the authorities to the manner in which we, as a nation, have dealt with the investment bankers, mortgage lenders, and hedge fund managers who wrecked the world economy and brought it to the precipice of depression.

In late November 2011, Federal District Court Judge Jed Rakoff rejected a proposed settlement between the Securities and Exchange Commission and Citigroup.[3] He found the proposed penalty of $285 million—without an admission of guilt—indefensible. Citibank is alleged to have intentionally misled customers into investing in mortgage back securities that they—Citibank themselves—were betting would fail. While there is some dispute regarding whether this is a public fraud—a determination that depends on the disclosure Citi made to its customers and, presumably, was the purpose of the investigation—the SEC apparently had a case sufficient to push Citigroup into settlement. For Citicorp, the effect of this "penalty" is miniscule.

This pattern of small settlement without admission of guilt is the rule, rather than the exception, for SEC enforcement actions,[4] and Rakoff takes issue with this. As he suggests in his opinion, "a consent judgment that does not involve any admissions and that results in only very modest penalties is just as frequently viewed, particularly in the business community, as a cost of doing business . . ."[5] That is, if Citigroup did what the SEC alleges, then the fine is shamefully small, the absence of an admission of wrong-doing shields Citigroup from the reputational costs of their behavior, and there is little or no effect of this "enforcement" action on shaping future behavior. Nothing in the public interest is accomplished.

Within hours of Judge Rakoff's decision, we learned from Bloomberg News[6] on the same day that Former Treasury Secretary Hank Paulson—appointed to that position directly from his role as CEO of Goldman Sachs by George W. Bush—"briefed" Wall Street investment barons and hedge fund managers in the summer of 2008 on the impending federal seizure of Fannie Mae and Freddy Mac on the very same day he told reporters from the *New York Times* that he expected federal audits to find that both companies were secure. If this allegation is true, it is the ultimate act of insider trading and could make the US government potentially liable for huge damages to the regular citizens who held common and preferred stock in those two companies.

Do you think Secretary Paulson is going to go to jail for this? Chances are there will be neither investigation nor indictment, much less prison time. In virtually every opportunity the Obama administration has had to investigate and prosecute the fraudulent behavior that led to our current economic circumstances, it hasn't. This should not be surprising. The weakening of both bank regulation and securities regulation was accomplished under the Clinton administration, and the architect of this reduced regulation—Larry Summers—was appointed by Obama to manage the nation's economy at precisely the moment his earlier efforts toward deregulation were allowing the economy to come flying apart.

Rather, the Obama administration's efforts have been to let Wall Street off the hook. An egregious example was their attempt to pressure states into accepting a weak settlement from mortgage lenders and investment banks that so richly profited from the real estate bubble and the ill-fated mortgage-backed securities. Only a few holdouts, like New York Attorney General Eric Schneiderman and a handful of his colleagues, showed a willingness to resist the administration's demands that the states go along with this hand-slap, particularly one that would indemnify these companies from further criminal investigation. In the end, the settlement reached in February of 2012 provided only $1,500 to $2,000 to individuals who lost their homes to foreclosure as a consequence of robo-signing and unverified documents, though the possibility of future civil and criminal action was preserved.[7]

I highlight these severely contrasting snapshots from American law enforcement to illustrate in the starkest possible terms how severely the American legal and political systems cater to the interests of the "1%" and are stacked against ordinary Americans. The ability of capitalism to reform itself is in serious doubt, a conclusion reluctantly concurred in by none other than market champion Alan Greenspan in testimony before Congress in October 2008 as the economy was collapsing.[8] Despite his apparent remorse, however, Greenspan's conclusion in that hearing again reiterated his faith in the self-correcting mechanisms of markets, whose failures to which he had just fessed up moments before notwithstanding:

> Whatever regulatory changes are made, they will pale in comparison to the change already evident in today's markets . . . Those markets for an indefinite future will be far more restrained than would any currently contemplated new regulatory regime.

The basis on which Greenspan reasserts his faith is, to say the least, elusive.

We witness a level of economic inequality today not seen since *prior* to the Great Depression. How unequal are we? "After decades of stability in the post-war period, the top decile share [of income] has increased dramatically over the last twenty-five years and has now regained its pre-war level. Indeed, the top decile share in 2007 is equal to 49.7 percent, a level higher than any other year since 1917 and even surpasses 1928, the peak of stock market bubble in the 'roaring' 1920s. In 2010, the top decile share is equal to 47.9 percent."[9]

Despite this alarming increase in inequality, there is no policy effort to reverse this trend. Rather, public policy today is formulated to advance corporate and financial interests that will worsen, not shrink, inequality. This is so because of the willingness—even enthusiasm—of the wealthy and financial interests to open their wallets to fund campaigns. And while we have witnessed the beneficence bestowed on GOP candidates, 527 groups and SuperPACS by folks such as Sheldon Adelson, Foster Friess, and the Koch brothers, we must also remember that senior leadership and employees of Goldman Sachs, JP Morgan Chase, Citigroup, UBS, and Morgan Stanley were in the top ranks of donors to Barack Obama's successful campaign in 2008.[10]

The degree to which the political and legal systems favor the wealthy and powerful is breathtaking in scope and arrogance. Nowhere is this more nakedly obvious than in GOP tax preferences. Claiming, falsely, that the current marginal tax rate is severely curtailing investment, the "fix" for this faux problem is tax cuts for the highest income earners. If the economy is growing or shrinking, in good times or bad, the preferred policy is the same. GOP fiscal "policy" then isn't policy at all but rather an article of faith, since it is invariant to social and economic conditions.

Fake crises are manufactured and phony solutions offered whose principal purpose is to strengthen the politics of the wealthy. For example, the faux problem of vote fraud (there is none) gives rise to Voter ID laws whose intended effect is to drive down voter participation of the poor, working class, and minority voters. Falsely blaming deficits on "over-compensated" public employees is used to justify the phony solution of union-busting legislation, whose intended effect is to defund and weaken one of the few powerful interest groups favoring the working class and poor. The fake issue of social security insolvency is the basis of the drive to privatize old-age pensions with the intended effect of putting billions in the pockets of investment banks and brokerage houses.

In recent years, we have witnessed the dramatic acceleration of this trend. The election of 2010, moving the US House and state legislatures and governors' mansions across the country into the GOP column, triggered a wave of coordinated policy attacks on public and private sector unions, immigrants, voting rights, and reproductive choice using copycat legislation. We have heard elected officials and candidates for President suggest that banks are *too* regulated, that child-labor laws are "stupid," that corporations are people with free speech rights that equate to unlimited campaign spending, that the EPA should be abolished, that the poor pay too little in taxes (and maybe shouldn't be allowed to vote), that Medicare should end, and that social security is an unconstitutional Ponzi scheme.

The Occupy movement has provided a rare moment of clarity, when our attention is drawn to the very raw deal that our government is providing us, and voices of working people have been raised in protest. The wealthy right, in turn, cries "class warfare" when they and their politicians have been responsible for a 60-year assault on the very reforms that saved capitalism from its excesses. With no apologies to Fukuyama, our future depends on the willingness of American workers to "re-start" history, to reject the political reality where the only choices at the ballot box are between crony capitalism and craven capitulation. They can begin this process by repeatedly and vigorously laying bare the true agenda of proposed legislation, and holding politicians of all stripes accountable for failing, in every way, to assure political and legal systems that are fair.

Political Remedies to
Economic Inequality

David D. Laitin

THE OCCUPY MOVEMENT HAS DRUMMED INTO our national consciousness the fact that our political process is delivering policies that mainly serve the interests of the top one percent of Americans. Evidence presented throughout this volume on the level of economic inequality that is barely remedied by current redistributive policies lends support to the fundamental claim of the movement. This raises a simple question: If democracy is a system designed to permit equal voice to everyone—indeed this is what we mean by political equality—why are we consistently ending up with policies that serve mainly the interests of the very rich?

One obvious answer is that political inequality in America supports economic inequality. The very rich, usually by embedding themselves in the capillaries of legislative power, have undue influence in elections and policy-making. This is a diagnosis of despair. However, there are institutional changes that would compel our representatives to pay more attention to the median voter than to corporate lobbyists or to the ultra-wealthy who fund their campaigns. Here I present two reforms that are in one sense utopian, but in another sense sufficiently concrete to allow for focused political action.

But first allow me to introduce readers to the median voter, and why democratic theory pays so much attention to this statistical concept.[1] The median voter is, by definition, that voter on some dimension who is exactly in the middle of the distribution of voters along that dimension. On the income dimension, for instance, assuming for arithmetic simplicity an odd number of voters, the median voter is that voter in the exact center of the income distribution. Any office seeker in a majoritarian system, in pure theory, would seek to attract this voter to his or her party, for this is the voter who determines the electoral winner.

In political science, a formal model predicts that the ideal point of the median voter (say, on the rate of redistribution of income) should be decisive for tax policy. The model predicts a tax rate (with a large set of assumptions including the ignoring of the deadweight loss incurred by taxation and an equal tax rate for all) measured as follows:

T_{pi} [preferred tax rate for redistribution by voter i]
$= 1-$ (voter i's income/mean income)

In a sense, this is the rate, should the median voter's ideal point win out, that maximizes its return from redistribution, i.e. delivers the highest income to the median voter after redistribution. The median voter is balancing the benefits of redistribution (the money redistributed to it) against the costs (the money taken from it in taxes).

DAVID D. LAITIN   139

Consider a few examples with an electorate of nine voters and with the median voter being voter i, to clarify the basic mathematical intuition in this formula. In Example 1, Table 1, there is moderate income inequality and mean income (that is, the sum of all income divided by number of income earners) is equal to the median income (that is, the level of income at exactly the middle of the income distribution). Under this condition, the median voter has no interest in redistributive taxation. The formula reveals this lack of interest. Here the median voter earns $50,000. We now take the median voter income ($50,000) divided by the mean income ($450,000 / 9 = $50,000), and subtract this from 1. The result is zero. The formula thereby predicts a preferred tax policy of zero (i.e., no taxation) when the median voter's income is equal to that of the median voter, and when the median voter's preferences rule.

Now let us look at the case closer to reality in the U.S. In Example 2, Table 1 there is income inequality with some very high flyers and a hollowed out middle class. Here, median income is far lower than the mean. In this second example, the median voter's income is still at $50,000. But here the mean income is $150,000. Inputting the figures into the formula, we get a preferred tax rate of [1-(50,000/150,000)] = 2/3 on all incomes for equal re-distribution to all voters. In this case, our median voter would face a tax of $33,333 (2/3 of $50,000). But when all citizens are taxed at this rate, the government collects $900,000 (2/3 of the total societal income of $1,350,000), to be distributed equally to all (i.e., $100,000 to each of the nine voters). Our median voter, with redistribution, would add this $100,000 to its retained $16,667, and would wind up with $116,667. Using the same calculation, our high flyer (who earned $500,000) would pay $333,333 in taxes and wind up with $266,666 after taxation and redistribution ($100,000 plus the retained $166,667). Meanwhile, his or her destitute fellow citizens (who earned $10,000) would each wind up with $106,667. The spread from the richest to the poorest, should the median voter's preferred tax rate prevail, would change after taxation and re-distribution from $490,000 to $160,000, surely a progressive shift.[2] This is the (theoretical) power of a democratic system that is responsive to the median voter! In sum, democratic theory predicts the greater the income of the mean voter relative to that of the median voter, the higher the rate of taxation for re-distribution, again favoring the interests of the median at the expense of the interest of the voter with the mean income.

Table 1: Median Voter Theorem Applied to Preferred Tax Rate

Ranking by Income	Example 1: Median Income = Mean Income	Example 2: Median Income < Mean Income
1	10	10
2	20	10
3	30	10
4	40	10
Median	50	50
6	60	185
7	70	275
8	80	300
9	90	500
[Mean Income]	50	150

Note: Incomes are listed in thousands of dollars.

How is this relevant to the issue of inequality in America, the focus of the Occupy movement? Consider Table 2, where the mean and median family incomes are reported (from the Census Bureau)[3] for 2010 as compared to a generation ago (in 1980). The fourth column reports the percentage of the mean family that is earned by the median family. We see that there is a growing drop in the ratio of median to mean family income (from 0.84 to 0.73), for which we should expect (in the median voter theorem) an increasing redistributive tax. Instead, we see (in column 5 of Table 2) that the highest marginal tax rate in 1980 was twice as high as that of 2010![4]

As income inequality in the United States has risen over the past generation (measured by the growing di-

Table 2: Household Income in the U.S. and Top Marginal Tax Rate

Year	Median Household Income	Mean Household Income	Median/Mean income	Top Marginal Tax Rate
1980	44,616	53,064	.84	70%
2010	49,445	67,530	.73	35%

Note: Income is in constant 2010 dollars.

vergence of the mean and median incomes), the basic models of democratic theory would consequently have predicted over this past generation greater pressures to tax the rich.[5] We should see, if the median voter theorem is correct, more pressure to redistribute through the tax rate. But in the United States, as we have seen, public policy has veered in an opposite direction. A political scientist wants to know why. We should expect some deviation from the ideal tax rate of the median voter in light of concerns over international competitiveness and providing incentives to the wealthy to seek the highest returns on their investments, such that our national wealth increases. However, the 35 percent marginal tax rate for the richest Americans is far lower than needed to give our high flyers incentives to invest. In this same period, the estate tax has been practically emasculated. As the rich are facing lower redistributive tax rates, low-skilled workers are getting less protection. In the past generation, the real value of the minimum wage has been allowed to fall (from $7.62 in 1980 to $7.25 in 2009, in constant 2009 dollars).[6]

Why should this be so? I now describe two sources of political inequality in America, each with remedies that ought to be part of Occupy's agenda for action.

First, our electoral institutions structurally and systematically disfavor the median voter.[7] Yes, we have a one-person-one-vote democracy, but at the federal level this core democratic principle is distorted by the manner in which our elected representatives are allocated across the population. The U.S. Senate, for instance, is constructed on the basis of equal representation by each state, regardless of the population of each state. Each California Senator represents some 19 million residents; each Senator from Wyoming represents about 280,000 residents, giving residents of Wyoming sixty-seven times the power to influence outcomes in the Senate than do those from California. In Congressional districting, our method of calculating legislative representation vastly underrepresents those living in urban centers where support for remedying economic inequality is strongest. This is due to the fact that the margin of victory in progressive urban constituencies is much larger than in conservative suburban districts. Consequently, more progressive votes are "wasted" than conservative ones.

It is the presidency, however, that is the big prize. For the presidency, a constitutional amendment giving victory to the winner of a majority of voters, and thereby empowering the median voter, would shift policy to a greater extent towards the ideal point of the median voter. This would involve eliminating the Electoral College—the archaic institution that gives each state votes that are the sum of its senators and representatives, thereby giving Wyoming voters more power than those from California. With majority rule, this inequity would be remedied.[8]

There is another advantage to a majority vote for the president. Because states like California and New York are barely contested, neither candidate spends much time in courting voters in these socially diverse states. This too would be remedied with the elimination of the electoral college system, as the return on campaign investment in large urban districts would be higher than with today's electoral rules, where candidates target their messages largely in suburban districts in a few states (like Ohio, Florida, New Mexico and New Hampshire) where a tiny number of voters can determine a large swath of delegates to the Electoral College. When candidates can win by attracting large numbers of voters in diverse states, as would happen if the majority of the entire country ruled, policies that would attract the median voter of the country are more likely to be advocated by the leading candidates.

Securing passage of a constitutional amendment to eliminate the Electoral College state-by-state may seem quixotic though several suggested half-measures have higher chances of legislative success. One proposal would award two "senatorial" electoral votes to the overall winner of a state and then a single electoral vote for the winner of each congressional district within a state.[9] Another scheme, called "The National Popular Vote Bill" would be an interstate compact in which each state would guarantee all its electoral votes to the candidate who receives the most popular votes in all 50 states (and DC).[10] Though each of these alternatives has its advantages and difficulties, both of them violate the fundamental concern of "Occupy," namely the equality of all voters. To be sure, the constitutional change that is implied by the elimination of the Electoral College will hit up against what political scientists call "veto points" every step of the way. But social movements ought to go for what is right, and not merely what is feasible. Any movement in support of the popular election of the President would be a persistent thorn in the side of those who want to preserve the unequal status quo.

Disenfranchisement is a second reason that our political institutions systematically favor the rich. Vast numbers of our workers at the subsistence level are taxed in America (if not by withholding taxes on salaries, then by sales taxes), but not represented. This is not wholly due to the complexities of registration, which deter many voters, most usually the poorer Americans. Nor am I referring here to felons and ex-felons (amounting to about 4 million disen-franchised citizens), who are disproportionately from households below the median income.[11] Here I refer to hard-working immigrants who are rendered politically mute by our current institutions.

Data collected by political scientists show that the standing of the median voter in the income distribution today is no worse than was true thirty years ago.[12] Can one infer, then, that the political process has worked more-or-less in line with democratic theory, in the narrow sense that the returns to redistribution to the median family has not declined over the past generation? The answer is "no," and this concerns immigration. From 1972 to 2000, the median *family* income of non-citizens fell from 82 percent of the median income of voters to 65 percent, while the fraction of the population that is non-citizen rose from 2.6 percent to 7.8 percent. Because non-citizens are poorer than citizens, mean resident income is less than mean citizen income. Non-citizens thus decrease the ratio of median to mean income, making stronger measures of redistribution less attractive to the median voter.

Throughout Europe, with much more progressive social policies, immigrants have the right to vote at the sub-national level. Indeed, several U.S. states (and those mostly with large immigrant populations) in the late 19th and early 20th centuries enfranchised non-citizens who had begun the process of naturalization, so there is precedent here at home.[13] Were this so in America today, local and state-level candidates would need to speak to immigrant interests, and be more open to such policies as minimum wage increases. If candidates at the state level had reason to be responsive to immigrants, because they were voters, politicians would have had second thoughts before proposing grievous anti-immigrant policies as have been passed in Alabama. Furthermore, since success at the national level requires first winning elections at the local or state level, a new voter-rights act at the state level enfranchising immigrants would increase the relative number of progressive officials seeking national office. Granting local voting rights (at the state level) as a complement to the legalization of the undocumented (at the national level) in a general immigration reform package would also help nurture policies that put a heavier burden of taxation on the rich. Granting voting rights to our immigrants, along with opening the polls to ex-felons and eliminating the complexities of registration, would enhance political equality in America. This is another battlefield, to be fought state by state, with political equality for all as the goal.

Critics of my two proposals will argue that the poor in America are often hoodwinked into voting for policies that favor the wealthy through ideological manipulation or the exploitation of "wedge issues" such as "family values."[14] (To be sure, Wall Street tycoons are equally blinded, pouring money into the political party that has consistently performed worse in protecting stock portfolios over the past century.)[15] However, on average the poor vote for more progressive policies, and increasing the voice of the poor, so that it approaches equal voice with the rich, is an important step in the right direction, even if it will never be a full remedy for the egregious inequality we now face.

Activism ought to be tied to goals. We should support a constitutional amendment for a popularly elected president and laws that grant political representation in local elections to our immigrant populations. Conventional Occupy-inspired critiques have legitimately focused on how money buys candidates or influence. Such critiques haven't focused enough on more narrowly numerical problems with how votes in the U.S. are tallied up and counted which, as we have seen, can have profound implications for our income distribution. My two concrete proposals, though elaborated in the mathematics of incentives and not in the psychology of rage, are in the spirit of Occupy and would play an important complementary role to Occupy's symbolic protests in challenging an unacceptable status quo.

State Millionaire Taxes

Cristobal Young and Charles Varner

THE OCCUPY MOVEMENT HAS FOCUSED PUBLIC attention on inequality in a way not seen in many years. National politics are stalled in seeming policy paralysis, but there is growing momentum for millionaire taxes at the state level. Since 2004, eight states have adopted a millionaire tax. The Occupy movement, with its nationwide grassroots presence, could push this policy to every state in the country. Modest change, modeled on current tax policy in New Jersey, would call for an extra 3 percent tax on the top 1 percent of earners. Legislatures can tailor tax brackets to the "Top One Percent" as defined in each state. In a federal system like ours, local policy can both complement and inform national policy agendas.

Inequality and Its Discontents

America has increasingly become what economists Robert Frank and Philip Cook labeled a "winner-take-all society," where the most successful competitors reap a disproportionate share of economic rewards.[1] The gap between the "winners" and everyone else has grown sharply in recent decades. In 2010, the top one percent of earners received 20 percent of all income, compared to just 9 percent of all income in 1970.[2] Since Nixon was president, the share of income flowing to the very top has more than doubled.

As the inequality of market rewards has grown, the federal income tax system has also tilted in favor of the top. Since 1980, the tax rate on the very highest salaries has been cut in half, from 70 percent to 35 percent. Meanwhile, profits from the buying and selling of financial assets (capital gains) are now treated as protected income and taxed at a much lower rate than income from salaries and wages (labor gains). The 13.9 percent tax rate Mitt Romney paid on over $20 million in income in 2010 is largely the result of this capital gains shelter. Moreover, most multi-million dollar estates now pay no taxes at all. The offspring of the very rich inherit their first $5 million completely tax free.

The vast majority of the public now supports higher taxes on the rich. 75 percent of people support raising taxes on Americans with incomes over $1 million per year.[3] As shown in Figure 1, so do most Republican voters and even most Tea Party supporters.

Figure 1. Popular Support for Millionaire Tax

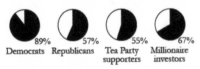

Sources: Data from Langer, ABC News/Washington Post Poll, Spectrum Group, Millionaire Corner survey, http://www.millionairecorner.com/article/economic-situation-warrants-tax-hikes-program-cuts-say-millionaires.

In fact, tax policy in America is so far out of sync with public values that even millionaires support higher taxes on the rich. Warren Buffett has been leading the charge, supported by the "Patriotic Millionaires" activist group. According to a survey by the investment group Spectrem, 67 percent of millionaire investors are in favor of a millionaire tax.

What holds federal tax reform back then is not a lack of popular support, but rather policy paralysis in Washington. A new millionaire tax would return America closer to its traditional post World War II tax policies. It would also move us closer to many of our international peers. For example, the "big four" European countries—Germany, France, Italy, and the United Kingdom—have top marginal rates on the wealthy ranging from 40 to 50 percent—all higher than the top rate in the United States.[4]

Fifty States: Room for Reform

How, then, to go forward? Given the last decade of declining tax progressivity, and a stalled Congress, we should look to the states to take incremental steps to a fairer tax system. New state taxation of the top one percent is a good starting point because state tax systems are generally quite regressive. States tend to rely heavily on sales taxes, and often have flat-rate income taxes. This means that lower-income people spend more of their household budgets on state taxes than do the wealthy.

In state-by-state analyses of tax shares—counting state and local income, property, sales, and excise taxes—the picture is stark. Every state has a regressive tax system. There is not a single state in America where the rich pay a greater share of their income in taxes than do the poor or the middle class. The rich do pay, but they pay a lower, and in many cases, much lower, overall rate.

How do state tax systems treat the 99 percent, compared to the top one percent? Figure 2 shows the states with the smallest and largest tax gaps. The states with the "most equal" tax systems are California, Vermont, and Delaware. Across these three states, the richest households pay 6.5 percent on average, only a little less than the average tax rate paid by everyone else (7.6 percent). Washington, Florida, and South Dakota, in contrast, have the "least equal" tax systems. Here, the richest households pay a tax rate of only 2.2 percent—dramatically less than the average tax rate on everyone else (9.5 percent). These are states that have no individual income taxes, and rely heavily on sales taxes to finance their state budgets. Appendix Table 1 shows these data for each state in the country.

In the face of these tax inequities, some states have initiated tax reform. In 2004, New Jersey passed a "millionaire tax," though it might be better labeled a "Top One Percent" tax.[5] The tax falls on those with incomes above $500,000, and as it happens, the cut-off for the top one percent of incomes in New Jersey is about $500,000. The tax struck a chord in this high-inequality era, and has been spreading. As shown in Table 1, seven other states have since passed their own versions of a millionaire tax.

Figure 2. States with Smallest and Largest Tax Gaps

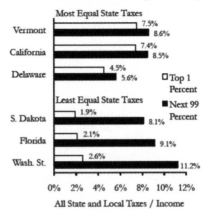

Most Equal State Taxes

Vermont — 7.5% / 8.6%
California — 7.4% / 8.5%
Delaware — 4.5% / 5.6%

☐ Top 1 Percent
■ Next 99 Percent

Least Equal State Taxes

S. Dakota — 1.9% / 8.1%
Florida — 2.1% / 9.1%
Wash. St. — 2.6% / 11.2%

0% 2% 4% 6% 8% 10% 12%

All State and Local Taxes / Income

Source: Davis et al. 2009.
Note: See Appendix Table 1 for data on all states.

Table 1. States with a Millionaire Tax

State	Year Passed	Top Bracket
New Jersey	2004	$ 500,000
California	2005	$ 1,000,000
Maryland	2008	$ 1,000,000
Hawaii	2009	$ 200,000
Wisconsin	2009	$ 225,000
Oregon	2009	$ 250,000
New York	2010	$ 500,000
Connecticut	2010	$ 500,000

Source: Tax Foundation, State Individual Income Tax Rates. 2011.

28 percent of the US population now lives in a state with a millionaire tax. There is much momentum for states to support their strained budgets with a modest tax increase on the very highest income earners.

No Flight of the Millionaires

The downside risk of a state millionaire tax, as critics repeatedly emphasize, is that it may become "the last straw" that convinces the richest households to pack their bags. It is much easier for people to move out of state than to move out of country. When Maryland passed its millionaire tax, critics panned it as the Get Out of Maryland Tax Act.[6] As New Jersey Governor Chris Christie said, "Ladies and gentlemen, if you tax them, they will leave."[7]

Actually, they do not. In a detailed study of New Jersey we drew on unique access to the state's complete income tax records over eight years, which gave us a virtual census of the state's millionaires.[8] After the millionaire tax was passed in 2004, there was a *surge* in the number of millionaires in New Jersey—

an increase of 38 percent (13,000 new millionaires). Of course, this spike was fueled by income growth at the top—more people *becoming* millionaires—rather than by in-migration. The tax happened to come in effect during the Wall Street boom, with soaring bonuses pushing many upper-middle class workers into the millionaire bracket.

In terms of actual millionaire migration, the effect of the new tax was close to zero. For every 2,000 millionaire households in the state, *one* household per year migrated in response to the tax. The total number of millionaire households lost over four years was 70. They took with them $16 million in foregone tax revenue. By contrast, the tax raises $1 billion per year.

New Jersey is a geographically tiny state, with a higher population density than Japan. Many New Jerseyans could move 30 miles or so and find themselves in the lower tax states of Connecticut or Pennsylvania. If a tax on the one percent is viable in the small state of New Jersey, it should be viable just about anywhere.

Arguments about millionaire migration have to face a reality that people develop strong and enduring attachments to where they live. People are reluctant to move because the costs of selling their home and moving elsewhere are very high (real estate brokerage fees for selling a house and buying a new one amount to about 25 percent of annual income, on average). They are attached to family and friends, and reluctant to take their kids out of school. They do not want to give up their local business connections and try to start over in a new state. On average, only about 1.5 percent of people change their state in any given year. Among people born in America, less than one-third change their state *at any point in their lives.*[9]

Top One Percent Taxes and Sound State Fiscal Policy

One real drawback of the millionaire tax is that its revenues are quite sensitive to the business cycle. The number of people earning more than $500,000 per year falls during recessions, creating a budget hole for states. The millionaire tax is much more sensitive to recessions than are sales or property taxes. Smart policy would call for 30 percent of revenues from the millionaire tax to be banked for a "rainy day" fund.

Perhaps a better option would be tying the millionaire tax to the state's unemployment rate. In good times, there would be a baseline millionaire tax of 1 percent. When a state's jobless rate rises above 6 percent, the millionaire tax rises to 3 percent. And when joblessness rises above 8 percent—a serious recession—the millionaire tax rises to 5 percent. This ties the extra taxes that millionaires pay to the state of the local economy, and helps ensure that wealth "trickles down" in hard times.[10]

The national story of budget crisis and austerity cuts plays out in nearly every state in the country. Since the economic meltdown began in September 2008, state and local governments have cut some 650,000 jobs—many of them in education. And after years of cuts, 29 states still face large budget gaps for fiscal year 2013, totaling $44 billion.[11] The need for revenues in most states ranges from serious to desperate.

In troubled times, taxing the rich is something even the one percent think is fair. With so many state governments in budget crisis around the country, a millionaire tax bill—"3% from the top 1%"—is a flexible and modest policy that should be on the table in every state. In this way, local democracy can provide a leadership for tax fairness at the national level.

Appendix Table 1. State and Local Tax Burdens

State	Income Percentile		State	Income Percentile	
	Top 1	Next 99		Top 1	Next 99
Ala.	4.0%	9.0%	Mont.	4.6%	5.8%
Alaska	2.2%	4.5%	N. Dak.	6.1%	9.8%
Ariz.	4.6%	9.4%	N. Mex.	4.5%	9.5%
Ark.	5.9%	11.0%	N.C.	6.8%	9.0%
Calif.	7.4%	8.5%	N.D.	4.3%	7.7%
Colo.	4.2%	8.0%	N.H.	2.0%	6.3%
Conn.	4.9%	9.9%	N.J.	7.4%	9.0%
Del.	4.5%	5.6%	N.Y.	7.2%	10.6%
Fla.	2.1%	9.1%	Nev.	1.6%	6.5%
Ga.	5.7%	10.2%	Ohio	6.4%	10.5%
Hawaii	6.3%	10.5%	Okla.	4.8%	8.7%
Idaho	6.3%	8.2%	Oreg.	6.2%	7.9%
Ill.	4.1%	10.2%	Pa.	3.9%	9.0%
Ind.	5.3%	10.1%	R.I.	5.6%	10.0%
Iowa	6.0%	9.8%	S. Dak.	1.9%	8.1%
Kans.	5.9%	8.7%	S.C.	5.5%	7.3%
Ky.	6.1%	9.8%	Tenn.	3.1%	8.9%
La.	5.2%	9.3%	Tex.	3.0%	8.7%
Mary.	6.2%	9.3%	Utah	4.9%	8.4%
Mass.	4.8%	9.3%	Va.	5.2%	8.1%
Md.	6.9%	9.5%	Vt.	7.5%	8.6%
Mich.	5.3%	9.1%	W. Va.	6.5%	9.1%
Minn.	6.6%	9.5%	Wash.	2.6%	11.2%
Miss.	5.5%	9.9%	Wis.	6.7%	10.0%
Mo.	5.4%	8.9%	Wyo.	1.5%	6.0%

Source: Oct 2009 permanent state and local income, property, sales, and excise taxes as share of 2007 income, for working-age filers, including federal deduction of state and local taxes (Davis et al. 2009).

The Politics of Occupy:
Now and Looking Ahead

Doug McAdam

THE OCCUPY PROTESTS HAVE BROUGHT WELCOME attention to various forms of inequality that characterize the contemporary United States. I too am deeply concerned by the extent and myriad forms of inequality that we see around us, but as a political analyst, I am just as worried by

•   the politics that have enabled these glaring inequities to develop over the past 30 years and which sustain them in the present;

•   the deep political divisions—the greatest since the Civil War—that have hollowed out our political institutions and undermined prospects for bipartisanship at the very moment we need it most desperately;

- and the very real threats to the viability of American democracy that are everywhere evident today.

Some of the essays in this volume focus on the first two of these concerns: the underlying political dimensions of persistent and growing inequality. I will confine myself to the final concern, describing the three "threats" to American democracy that I see as the most pressing.

The first of these threats is the corrupting influence of individual wealth and corporate money in the electoral process. This is hardly a new problem, of course, nor a peculiarly American one. The rich have always sought to use their wealth to shape politics to their advantage. But the stark material divide that now characterizes the U.S. makes the problem that much worse. The rich simply have that much more capacity to buy political influence than the rest of us. Societies can, of course, seek to insulate electoral politics from the influence of money by imposing constraints on who can donate to campaigns and in what amounts. However, by ruling in the 2010 case, *Citizens United v. Federal Election Commission*, that restrictions on corporate giving to electoral campaigns constitutes a violation of the constitutional right of free speech, the Supreme Court effectively removed whatever safeguards existed in this regard, making it that much easier for wealthy individuals and corporations to bend the political system to their will through campaign contributions.

The 2010 mid-term elections brought with it another, more idiosyncratic, threat to democracy: the narrow ideological commitment of several dozen new Tea Party-backed Republican Congressmen determined to eviscerate the "socialistic" Federal government. This development has already resulted in the "debt ceiling" debacle of last summer and contributed to the failure of the so-called Congressional "Super Committee" to reach agreement on a plan to cut the federal deficit by another $1.2 trillion. In the latter instance, the sticking point was once again the "threat" of new taxes on the richest individuals and corporations in the U.S.; taxes that some two-thirds of the American public support. The failure of the committee to reach consensus on such a plan triggered another $1.2 trillion in automatic cuts, many to entitlement programs already ravaged by earlier rounds of spending cuts.

In the end, however, nothing threatens the viability and vitality of American democracy more than extreme inequality itself. One of the guiding principles shaping U.S. foreign-aid policy for decades has been that economic development is a necessary prerequisite for the establishment of viable democracies in the developing world. Absent a decent standard of living and a reduction in extreme material disparities, the prospects for democracy are thought to be poor. And yet, rarely if ever, have we heard the extreme inequalities that have come to characterize the U.S. described as a threat to the health and well being of democratic practices here. But they certainly are.

I have already highlighted one way in which severe financial inequality threatens our democratic practices and ideals: the unchecked influence of individual wealth and corporate money on our electoral system. But there are many others. For example, gross material disparities clearly contribute to the growing "civic gap" in this country—that is, a dramatic imbalance in the rates of civic participation—especially among young minorities whose shared cynicism, pessimism and distrust of politics has reached epidemic proportions.[1] When large and growing segments of society lose faith in the fairness and legitimacy of the political system, the claim that we are a vibrant, healthy democracy rings hollow. What Jonathan Kozol called the "savage inequalities" that characterize K-12 schooling in the contemporary U.S. pose yet another clear threat to democracy. Even as we celebrate the U.S. as the birthplace of public education, we would do well to remember that the proponents of the idea saw schools as *civic* institutions as much as vehicles of individual advancement. But decades of deep cuts to educational budgets have undermined the civic function of the great majority of the schools serving disadvantaged youth.

Where does this leave us? The litany of our society's inequities and their distorting effects on our nominal democracy are daunting. Are they too entrenched, too daunting to change? Absolutely not.

To the extent that they are products of specific political trends that stretch back 30 years, they are amenable to change through countervailing political processes. And what might those political processes look like? As the chapter by David Laitin suggests, changes to certain political institutions and processes themselves—changes that would make our elected officials more responsive to the average citizen rather than the siren song of monied interested—are important. And of course the political effort should include conventional attempts to elect representatives at all levels of government who are committed to reversing the social, economic and political trends of the past few decades.

That said, significant social change has *never* been achieved in this country by conventional politics alone. From the outset, the American system was designed to insulate the federal government from radical change. As revolutionaries go, the founding fathers were deeply ambivalent and conflicted. They prized stability over all else, including any pretense to an egalitarian democracy. Whatever progress we have made in moving the country closer to this ideal has been slow, grudging, fragile and, most importantly, achieved during periods of broad progressive ferment by movements that challenged the system from below. Make no mistake about it; all the movements our textbooks now celebrate as part of America's glorious democratic heritage—from abolition to women's suffrage, to the labor movement, to the African-American freedom struggle—were fiercely resisted by the political and economic elite of the day. And while we're at it, let's do away with one more myth. American history should not be read as an inevitable progression toward a more just and equal union. Indeed owing to the trends of the last 30 years, we are, in many respects, farther from that ideal than we were three or four decades ago. It will take another period of progressive ferment and the building of new coalitions across racial, class and regional lines to restore balance to this country, re-dress the deep inequities that have been allowed to develop, revitalize democratic practices, and restore faith in the ideal of a just society.

All well and good; but what should such a move-ment look like? Judging from the many skeptics and critics of the Occupy protests, one popular answer is that any sustained movement will need to have more structure, leaders and narrowly focused goals than the effort to date. With the possible exception of the is-sue of goals, I couldn't disagree more with this line of criticism. I see these features of the Occupy effort neither as liabilities nor as atypical of most of the broad, progressive, movements mentioned above. The great majority of these movements had no central-ized, hierarchical structure or single, unitary leader. The image of the "charismatic leader" understand-ably shapes the popular conception of social movements. But leaders such as Martin Luther King, Jr., or Gandhi are exceedingly rare in the annals of sustained progressive movements. And even in King's case, it would be inaccurate to say that he was *the* leader of the modern civil rights movement. Not only were there many other notable leaders in the struggle, but more importantly, there was no singular movement that any one person could have led. The movement was, in fact a coalition of countless local efforts, spanning several decades, hundreds of discrete groups, and making use of all manner of strategies and tactics—legal, illegal, institutional, non-institutional, violent, non-violent. Without discounting King's importance, it would be sheer fiction to call him the leader of what was fundamentally an amorphous, fluid, dispersed movement.

We tend to think of movements as akin to organizations—that is, as unified, bounded entities pursuing specified goals under the leadership of specific individuals. Biased by this conventional understanding, we see even sympathetic observers of the Occupy protests urging a pursuit of specific goals using the tactics and organizational structures that make the most sense to us. But given all that the Occupy protests have accomplished and continue to accomplish, why should those groups morph into the movement that you or I want to see? All broad, successful movements start somewhere, with a particular campaign or set of actions serving as the opening wedge. The Occupy protests have served that function, changing the conversation in this country, and creating space—literally and figuratively—within which others can act. The challenge for those of us who identify with the protests is to organize ourselves using whatever structures and towards whatever specific goals we see as consistent with the broader struggle. Before we can begin to characterize the generalized Occupy ferment as a movement, many others will need to begin to act in its name. In light of the economic and political stakes, this is a challenge worthy of our efforts.

VI

The Social Costs of Inequality

Capitalism Versus the Environment
Paul R. Ehrlich and Anne H. Ehrlich

As far as we know, our hunter-gatherer ancestors lived in relatively egalitarian societies that had no chiefs or kings, only leaders of the moment for war parties, dispute settlements, hunting expeditions, and so on. The capitalist economic system so dominant today traces back to the agricultural revolution, when families first became sedentary, were able to produce more food than they consumed, and thus get income by trading and thereby accumulate wealth. That crucial change laid the groundwork for a division of labor that led to priests, soldiers, politicians, commissars, rulers, shopkeepers, and eventually to modern capitalism with its entrepreneurs, Wall Street parasites, scientists, and a period of unprecedented growth in the human enterprise. A combination of markets, private ownership of the means of production, accumulation of capital, and the organization of corporations has led to enormous riches for the few and prosperity for a substantial minority of humanity.

But a dark side of capitalism—collusion among capitalists (anticipated by Adam Smith), and an insane belief that physical economies can grow forever—has gotten humanity into a predicament that civilization may not survive. Belief in the myth of perpetual economic growth is endemic to both politicians and second-rate economists as well as to most businesspeople in socialist as well as capitalist societies. Yet, in an era in which populations are approaching or have reached zero or negative growth in most industrialized nations, the justification for rapid material expansion in those economies is fading. At the same time, warning signs of material resource depletion are proliferating. Along with a failure to reduce population growth globally and to use resources prudently and equitably, that blind faith in perpetual growth has led to today's extraordinarily dangerous global environmental situation.

In the United States, the dilemma we face is exacerbated by the role of moneyed interests in politics, which support a powerful and effective disinformation machine programmed to lie about environmental threats.[1] This machine has, for example, perpetuated the myth that the famous 1972 "Limits to Growth" study was totally wrong,[2] when in fact its predictions—that complex feedbacks between different subsystems of the world economy such as agriculture, health, and industry, compounded by delayed responses, would lead to collapse—were remarkably accurate.[3] In the predicament we face today, the most immediate threats are to poor people and poor nations, although in the end, all of us will pay.

Human beings have always been small-group animals; they evolved genetically and culturally to deal with at most a few hundred individuals. Now civilization confronts a largely unrecognized emergency requiring it to quickly design a global governance and economic system that is far more equitable, suitable for a population of billions, *and* sustainable on a finite planet. Our planet is now so overpopulated that it would take about one and a half Earths to support today's population indefinitely—even with several billion people condemned to miserable lives.[4] Given that 2.5 billion more people are scheduled to be added to the population by 2050, a business-as-usual course would require conservatively about two planets; "conservatively" because non-linearities in the population-resource-environment relationship would cause disproportionate environmental destruction. Perhaps more to the point, something like *five* more planets would be required to support permanently today's global population at the average American lifestyle, and many economists seem to think that the US level of per-capita consumption should not only be spread around the globe, but should *increase*.

Driven to a large degree by the growth-requiring aspects of capitalism, humanity is exhausting its natural capital: deep agricultural soils, fossil groundwater, and the biodiversity that runs its life-support systems.[5] It is disrupting the climate, spreading toxic chemicals from pole to pole, increasing the chances of vast epidemics, and risking nuclear war over resources, especially water.[6] Many scientists fear that at most a decade or two remain to revolutionize our energy-mobilizing systems (still extremely dependent on fossil fuels) and revise our agriculture and water-handling systems to be flexible in the face of centuries of changing precipitation patterns.[7] Any chance of growing enough food to give a decent diet to all of *today's* population requires success in these endeavors. Furthermore, in a world riddled with inequality, the prosperity of all is threatened by the possibilities of nuclear or biological terrorism.

The growth of information and the siloing of expertise have led to today's *culture gap*—where even a well-educated person can be familiar with only an extremely tiny part of their society's non-genetic in-formation. In societies as complex as ours, it would be impossible to bridge the entire gap. Even so, edu-cation could close critical parts of it by imparting a basic understanding of the failures of civilization to treat either its environment properly or its citizens equitably. The culture gap is arguably one of the prime causes of the public's relative lack of concern over crucial environmental problems.[8]

Consider some of the intertwined ominous trends that are barely covered in the media.[9] The concentrations of greenhouse gases in the atmo-sphere have continued to increase, especially over the past half-century. The feedbacks recently dis-covered in the climate system have mostly been positive; that is, the warming itself is causing more warming.[10] One important feedback has been the reduction of Arctic sea ice in summer, which means that less of the sun's energy is reflected back into space, making the ocean warmer and further shrink-ing the ice cover.

In addition, ever more signs of climate disruption have appeared, from the accelerating flow of glaciers into the sea to an increased frequency of extreme weather events such as severe droughts, floods, and tornados. The Himalayan "water tower," the ice and snow of the Himalayas and the Tibetan Plateau, is also melting, which is likely first to cause a complex pattern of flooding and then drying of several major rivers that supply agricultural water to much of southern and eastern Asia.[11] That's the home of 1.6–2.0 billion people, with more being added all the time. Rising temperatures further threaten the food supply of those nations by reducing the yields of critical crops such as rice and wheat. Three of those countries are nuclear powers, and India and Pakistan each have many people who would like to go to war with the other country. A "small" nuclear exchange between them, say over a water dispute, could end civilization.[12]

Extinctions of populations and species, now occurring at a rate thousands or more times beyond baseline levels (rates during periods outside of the five prehistoric "mass extinctions"), make it continually clearer that humanity is causing a sixth mass extinction episode.[13] That means that working parts of human life-support systems, which supply critical ecosystem services such as nutrient cycling and soil replenishment, crop pollination, pest control, climate amelioration, and supplying fresh water, are being degraded. Almost a billion people have too little food, twice as many as when the Green Revolution technology was first deployed a half-century ago. That indicates that the number of immune-compromised individuals is also at record levels, making civilization's epidemiological environment more threatening. Along with other health consequences of the population explosion, the probability of deadly pandemics emerging is increasing.[14]

Subtle but frightening symptoms in human and some wildlife populations, such as an increased incidence of some cancers, birth defects, and developmental anomalies, are traceable to widespread exposure to hormone-disrupting chemicals and other toxic substances.[15] These pose increasing reasons for concern as more is learned about how early exposure to bioactive chemicals can influence development and survival. Besides assaulting many species that are themselves components of our life-support systems, toxics could be shifting the human sex ratio, causing developmental problems in children, and possibly reducing sperm counts. But these trends also remain mostly unrecognized, and little has been done to curb the growth-driven releases of potentially toxic substances into the environment.

Finally, racism and sexism are barriers to achieving sustainability, and progress in eradicating them has been far too slow and uneven. For instance, more gender equity could help limit population growth and thus improve the chances of maintaining an adequate food supply. The more rights and opportunities women have, the fewer children they want and produce.[16] A more gender, racially, and economically equitable world not only could greatly reduce the number of hungry and destitute people, it would help lower the numbers being added to an already overpopulated planet. It would also allow for a more universally educated global population.

An educated population will be needed, because governments and economic systems clearly must be redesigned to replace capitalism's growth imperative, rescale society, and internalize most externalities. Everyone needs to recognize that an under-regulated capitalism simply has not and cannot generate the sustainable redistribution of access to resources and the material and population shrinkage that will be essential in order to create an environmentally sound and reasonably equitable global society.[17] The challenge is immense and unprecedented.

Overcoming resistance from groups invested in unconstrained capitalism will require international cooperation, which won't likely be achieved without new institutions and a broad increase in social justice. And that will require what the Occupy movement apparently desires: for us to step back and ask "what are people for?" and consider whether the society we've built is truly the one we want. We have no choice but to address the challenge of meeting human needs in a constrained environment. Either humanity will change its ways, or they will be changed for us.

*The Rising Toll of Inequality on
Health Care and Health Status*

Donald A. Barr

WHILE THE TOP ONE PERCENT OF EARNERS IN
the U.S. were doubling their share of total income in
the past decade, middle- and lower-income families
were getting hit twice: in the face of falling household incomes, millions were also losing their access
to affordable health insurance. Rapidly rising health-
care costs coupled with expanding job losses have left
millions of American families exposed to potential
economic crisis when faced with illness or injury.
The number one cause for bankruptcy in the US is
an unexpected health crisis. The following statistics
tell the story.

Between 2001 and 2011, the average cost of employer-provided family health insurance coverage rose from $7,061 to $15,073—an increase of 113 percent. As health care costs continued to rise even in the face of a recession, employers shifted a growing share of the cost of insurance coverage onto the worker. The share of the health insurance premium paid by the worker went from $1,787 to $4,129, an increase of 131 percent. At the same time the share paid by the employer went up 108 percent, from $5,269 to $10,944.[1]

Workers not only had to pay more for their health insurance, but the value of that coverage declined as well. Between 2003 and 2010, the average deductible attached to employer provided health coverage increased 83 percent for families and 98 percent for individuals.[2] Out-of-pocket spending to cover the deductible and other costs not covered by health insurance increased by 74 percent over and above the higher contribution workers made to obtain that coverage.[3]

A major factor in the shift of health costs from employer to employee has been the rapid rise of what are often referred to as "Consumer Directed Health Plans" (CDHP). These types of plans offer workers traditional health insurance coverage that takes effect only after the employee has spent a specified amount out of pocket for health care each year. To qualify for tax-favored treatment, this annual deductible amount must be at least $1,200 for an individual and $2,400 for a family—thus the alternative name for these plans: "high deductible health plans" (HDHP). To help meet these higher deductibles, employees are offered the opportunity to set funds aside tax-free in either a health savings account (often held by a bank) or a health reimbursement account (typically administered by the employer). The employee can then use the funds in these accounts to pay directly for the costs of health care up to the amount of the deductible.

The theory behind these plans is that that when the employee is initially responsible for paying for care with his or her own money, s/he will be more selective in the type of care sought, thus reducing the overall cost of care. This outcome was confirmed in 1981 when the results of the original Rand Health Insurance Experiment were published.[4] However, those results also demonstrated that, while employees faced with the higher deductible use less care overall, they appear to be unable to distinguish between care that is medically necessary and care that is less important, foregoing both types of care at about the same rate.

Recent studies have confirmed this finding. As described in 2011 by Haviland et al, CHDP plans are associated with, "significant reductions in overall spending that increase with the level of the deductible… However, enrollment in CDHPs also leads to reductions in care that is considered beneficial for all groups, and this may have greater health consequences for lower income and chronically ill people than for others."[5] In a study of families with at least one member with a chronic medical condition, Galbraith et al. found that the frequency of "delayed/

foregone care due to cost is higher for both adults and children in HDHPs than in traditional plans. Families with lower incomes are also at higher risk for delayed/foregone care."[6]

Between 2006 and 2011, the number of workers nationally enrolled in CDHPs grew from 4 percent of those receiving employment-based insurance to 17 percent.[7] Among those working for small firms, 23 percent of covered workers were in HDHPs. It thus appears that, as a direct consequence of rising economic inequality:

1. Workers are paying an increasing share of the rapidly rising cost of employer-provided health insurance;

2. Over and above the cost of maintaining coverage, workers are paying an increasing amount for health care out of pocket; and

3. Many workers, especially those in small firms, are shifting to CDHPs in which they often end up foregoing otherwise needed care in an effort to reduce out of pocket costs.

DONALD A. BARR 199

These statistics, however, are for those families who have been able to maintain their health coverage during the era of rising economic inequality. With the unemployment rate more than doubling between 2007 and 2010, many other families lost their health insurance altogether. While some of the newly unemployed qualify for Medicaid or other public coverage, 1.1 million Americans became uninsured for every one-point rise in the unemployment rate.[8] Between 2007 and 2010, the number of uninsured adults in the U.S. went from 34.9 million to 41.2 million—an increase of nearly 20 percent.[9] Fortunately, due to expanded public coverage programs for children, the number of uninsured children actually went down slightly.

As might be expected, the loss of health insurance as a result of the falling economy fell disproportionately on low-income families. Of the 6.3 million people who became uninsured between 2007 and 2010, 5.6 million were in households earning less than 200 percent of the federal poverty line. As African Americans are disproportionately represented among low-income households, the risk of becoming uninsured for African Americans was nearly twice that of non-Hispanic whites.

During periods of rising inequality, inequities in the cost of health care and access to health insurance are only part of the story. Economic inequality also brings with it inequality in health outcomes that is independent of access to health care. A 25-year-old American with income more than four times the poverty level will live, on average, five years longer than a 25 year old with income less than twice the poverty line. Those with a college education are three times as likely to report excellent or very good health status as those of the same age who did not finish high school.[10] Those with less than a high school education are twice as likely to experience coronary heart disease as those of the same age who have graduated from college.[11] Money buys not just more life but a healthier life as well.

The association of economic disadvantage and worse health status is not unique to the U.S. Even in countries with universal health insurance, those with lower incomes experience higher rates of disease and reduced life expectancy. This is true in Canada, where individuals with lower incomes and less education had worse health outcomes, despite having a somewhat higher rate of using medical care than those with higher incomes.[12] It is also true in England, where for several decades the Whitehall Study has been documenting the health disadvantage of lower occupational status among fully employed civil servants, all with full access to health care in the British National Health Service.[13]

In the US we also find disturbing health disparities among different racial and ethnic minority groups, even when controlling for income and education. At all levels of education, black men and women on average report worse health than non-Hispanic whites of the same gender and level of education. Similarly, the average additional life expectancy of a 25-year-old black American is between two and four years shorter than a 25-year-old white American with the same level of income.[14]

The rising level of economic inequality in recent years has had a devastating impact both on the health and on the access to affordable health care of middle- and lower-income American families. Efforts to reverse the growth of inequality must identify policy approaches that will both constrain the rising cost of health care and expand its availability. Parallel to these efforts, we must also identify ways to aid those Americans who would otherwise suffer declining health and shorter life spans as a consequence of this inequality.

The Patient Protection and Affordable Care Act (ACA) signed by President Obama in 2010 will take a major step towards reducing the impacts of economic inequality on access to health care. Through an expansion of Medicaid, all individuals with incomes less than 133 percent of the poverty line who are citizens or permanent residents will gain health insurance coverage. Those in households between 133 percent and 400 percent of the poverty line will be able to take advantage of federal subsidies for the purchase of health insurance through newly established Health Benefit Exchanges.

As the data cited above suggests, though, expanding access to health insurance is only a partial solution to the adverse health impacts of rising inequality. As described by Woolf and Braveman, "Health disparities by racial or ethnic group or by income or education are only partly explained by disparities in medical care. Inadequate education and living conditions—ranging from low income to the unhealthy characteristics of neighborhoods and communities—can harm health through complex pathways. Meaningful progress in narrowing health disparities is unlikely without addressing these root causes."[15]

Rising economic inequality increases the cost of health care, reduces access to health insurance, and exacerbates the many social factors that contribute to disparities in length of life and quality of life. As the country struggles to escape the continuing drag of the recession, we must be vigilant in assuring that the policy solutions we adopt do not result in even wider economic inequality. Such inequality would only bring with it even worse disparities in the health of Americans.

VII

Inequality and Culture

Occupy Your Imagination
Michele Elam and
Jennifer DeVere Brody

Poetry is not a luxury.
—Audre Lorde[1]

FROM THE STREET POSTERS AND PERFORMANCE art, to pop-up galleries, giant light shows, poetry readings and micro-plays, the expressive arts are a fundamental component of the Occupy movement.[2]

The movement's new wave of organic creative expression revives the idea of art as necessity for an engaged citizenry. This is not self-referential art for art's sake—art that pleases only the artist. Rather,

An image of U. C. Davis police officer John Pike copied onto Pablo Picasso's "Guernica" [3]

this is timely art—art of and for the times—that is self-consciously responsive to immediate social concerns. Occupy has re-established art as a unique vehicle for social analysis and collective action that is as important to understanding—and potentially reshaping—the world around us as are the economic and sociological studies inspired by the movement.

There are already a great many archives documenting the art of the Occupy movement, including the Smithsonian, Occuprint.org, and Occupennial. org. These growing collections reveal a consistent concern with both the politics of art and the art of politics. They draw our attention not only to their content (such as the U.C. Davis cop who pepper-sprayed peaceful protesters on campus and now has been collaged into numerous classic paintings and photographs) but also to the places and conditions under which such political art can be produced. The art-activist group Occupy Museums, which has organized to protest the "cultural elitism" of the art world, has an antecedent in the 1970s Art Workers' Coalition (AWC), which was, in turn, inspired by Black Power and student activism. As art critic Ben Davis notes, AWC advanced demands not dissimilar to some of the first rumblings from Occupy Museums: expanded support for artists and artists' rights, more democratic museum structures that addressed New York's diverse communities, more attention for women artists and artists of color, less corporate influence on museum boards, and support for progressive causes like environmentalism and the antiwar movement.[4]

AWC used Picasso's "Guernica" (1937), which captured the bombing of civilians during the Spanish Civil War, to protest the Vietnam War by holding up

Members of the Art Workers' Coalition holding up copies of their "And babies" in from of "Guernica" [5]

their "And babies" poster in front of the painting at the The Museum of Modern Art (MOMA) in New York City. This anti-war statement, captured in a much-circulated photograph, is granted moral legitimacy and gravitas by this laying of art on art. But it is important to recognize that "Guernica" does not mystically transfer importance to the AWC poster by proximity, by the protesters simply placing an image in front of the artistic masterpiece. Rather, this palimpsest of art on art invites viewers to reflect differently on both the "old" and the "new" art and on the protests they represent. The juxtaposition of art across time, and across "high" and "low" genres, makes freshly relevant Picasso's painting even as it deepens the historical relevancy of AWC's poster. The civilian casualties of the Spanish Civil War resonate for a new generation, and the tragedies of the Vietnam War, seen in the light of Picasso's canonized images of human suffering and struggle, are made the more poignant by being placed within this richer context. Taken together, these images suggest a cycle of injustice and resistance that is greater than that found in either political event or artistic work considered alone.

Importantly, the site for this social-artistic protest was not on the street but in a museum, in the house of art. AWC transformed MOMA from a "cultured" space set apart from politics—where the touring "Guernica" hung on prestigious exhibit seemingly removed from political urgencies—to a space as appropriate and accessible as any other for everyday civil resistance.

MICHELE ELAM & JENNIFER DEVERE BRODY   213

Far outside museum walls, the 2011 meme of the pepper-spraying police lieutenant grafted onto "Guernica" and replicated on the Internet endlessly multiplies the sites and scenes of resistance. And perhaps even more provocatively than the AWC action at MOMA, the policeman meme is integrated into the painting's style. His image is not simply superimposed on "Guernica" but becomes part of its composition and thus is more deeply intertwined with and implicated in the historical abuse of power that the painting documents. Beyond AWC, one can find many similar echoes in today's movement from past artist-activism, such as Yayoi Kusama's 1968 "Naked Demonstration at Wall St." whose press release for the event read: "Stock is Fraud."[6]

One source that galvanized the Occupy movement came from the editors of ADBUSTERS, a magazine that criticizes consumerism using "mock" advertisements that at first glance look like the corporate promotions that litter our urban landscapes and television screens. ADBUSTERS issued a call on

Twitter that read "#occupywallstreet." This hashtag was accompanied by an image of a white female ballet dancer poised precariously on top of a raging bull that was meant to reference the out-of-control bull market. Despite the high culture elitism inherent in the image of the ballerina, it is significant that the juxtaposition to the irresponsible, self-enriching financial sector was a figure from the art world.

The oeuvre of Occupy embodies the idea that art is activism.

A major theme in many of the Occupy posters, exhibitions, and performances is inequality. The works highlight not only racial, sexual and economic inequities; but also critical questions about who is allowed to speak, lend an ear, or take the stage in the first place. Writer and activist W.E.B. Du Bois was among many who recognized that for people of color and the marginalized in general, art is an especially potent vehicle for social change. Creating the art is not enough, he insisted: the critical gatekeepers of art—the movie reviewers, the book editors, scholars and the theatre-owners—need to change how art is defined and disseminated.[7]

Occupy has been very effective, however, at bypassing the institutionalization and corporatization of art. With important exceptions, Occupy artwork has been made in the spirit of participation—not in private studios, not hosted by museums, nor sponsored by official agencies, but instead created and displayed through acts of collaborative protest in the spirit of a public march or demonstration.

Some have criticized the Occupy art as crude, propagandistic or, conversely, pointless. And still others dismiss the work for being either too humorous or too angry to count as "true" art. Some of these criticisms are legitimate but they do not de-legitimize the importance of Occupy art. In fact they illustrate and underscore artists' ability to spark debates about the value of free speech and the valuation of artistic expression. An even more radical understanding of art sees it not as a separate realm—nor even as an object set apart from society—but rather as a "do-

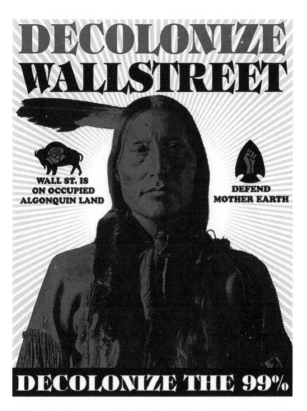

Ernesto Yerena

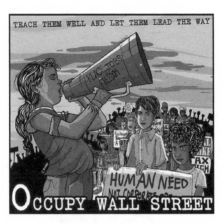

Christy C. Road

ing," that itself enacts change in the imagination and the world.

As noted, the oeuvre of Occupy embodies the idea that art is activism. Its artist-activists have emerged spontaneously across the world and join a historically deep and global community of painters, writers, performers, musicians and others—from novelist Sinclair Lewis to graphic artist Ai WeiWei, from singer Paul Robeson to visual artist Lorna Simpson—whose work has shaped the cul-

Mike Huynh

tural imagination that effects social justice. The imagination is the fulcrum of change as the anonymous graffiti artists of the Roman Empire knew as well.[8] Collectively, such activist-artworks make a revolutionary call: to create a better world, you must first occupy your imagination.

What if We Occupied Language?
H. Samy Alim

"We challenge language. We transform language. We remain aware of all of the resonances of the language we use."

–Angela Davis, Washington Square Park, October 30, 2011

IN THE LAST YEAR ALONE, THE OCCUPY MOVEMENT has transformed public spaces and institutions around the world, from the shutting down of ports in Oakland, California to the nearly year-long occupation of the Hong Kong and Shanghai Banking Corporation (HSBC) in China ('Occupy Central'). But the Occupy movement not only transformed public space, it transformed the public discourse as well.

Occupy.

For over a year, it has been nearly impossible to hear the word and not think of the Occupy movement. In fact, linguists noted *occupy*'s influence in January 2012 when the American Dialect Society overwhelmingly voted for it as the 2011 Word of the Year in Portland, Oregon. As Ben Zimmer, Chair of the New Words Committee of the American Dialect Society, noted: "It's a very old word, but over the course of just a few months it took on another life and moved in new and unexpected directions, thanks to a national and global movement...The movement itself was powered by the word."[1]

Occupy succeeded in shifting the terms of the debate, taking phrases like "debt-ceiling" and "budget crisis" out of the limelight and putting terms like "inequality" and "greed" squarely in the center. This discursive shift has made it more difficult for Washington to continue to promote the spurious reasons for the financial meltdown and the unequal outcomes it has exposed and further produced.

To most, the irony of a progressive social movement using the term "occupy" to reshape how Americans think about issues of democracy and equality has been clear. After all, it is generally nations, armies and police who occupy, usually by force. And in this, the United States has been a global leader. The American government has only just recently, after nearly a decade, ended its overt occupation of Iraq, and is still entrenched in Afghanistan while it maintains troops on the ground in dozens of countries worldwide. The United States also continues to be a staunch supporter of what is perhaps the most controversial occupation in contemporary history—the Israeli occupation of Palestine. All this is not to obscure the fact that the United States as we know it came into existence by way of occupation—a gradual and devastatingly violent one that all but extinguished entire Native American populations across thousands of miles of land. The linguistic irony could not be greater.

Yet in a very short time, this movement dramatically changed how we think about occupation. In early September, "occupy" signaled on-going military incursions. It also fit nearly into the capitalist framework, meaning "a job" or "a profession." Now the word signifies progressive political protest. It's no longer primarily about force of military power; instead it signifies standing up to injustice, inequality and abuse of power. It's no longer used just to define one's place in the machinery of capitalism; it's about reinvigorating the language of anti-capitalist movements.

In this sense, The Occupy movement has occupied language, has made occupy its own. And, importantly, people from diverse ethnic, cultural and linguistic backgrounds have participated in this linguistic occupation—it is distinct from both the history of forcible occupation and the force of historic capitalism in that it is built to accommodate all, not just the most violent or powerful.

What if we transformed the meaning of *occupy* yet again? Specifically, what if we thought of Occupy Language as more than the language of the Occupy movement, and began to think about it as a movement in and of itself? What kinds of issues would Occupy Language address? What would taking language back from its self-appointed "masters" look like? We might start by looking at these questions from the perspective of race and discrimination, and answer with how to foster fairness and equality in that realm.

Occupy Language might draw inspiration from both the way that the Occupy movement has reshaped definitions of "occupy," which teaches us that we give words meaning and that discourses are not immutable, *and* from the way indigenous movements have contested its use, which teaches us to be ever-mindful about how language both empowers and oppresses, unifies and isolates. For starters, Occupy Language might first take a reflexive look inward. In a recent interview, Julian Padilla of the People of Color Working Group pushed the Occupy movement to examine its linguistic choices:

> To occupy means to hold space, and I think a group of anti-capitalists holding space on Wall Street is powerful, but I do wish the NYC movement would change its name to "'decolonise Wall Street'" to take into account history, indigenous critiques, people of colour and imperialism... Occupying space is not inherently bad, it's all about who and how and why. When white colonizers occupy land, they don't just sleep there over night, they steal and destroy. When indigenous people occupied Alcatraz Island it was (an act of) protest.

This linguistic change can remind Americans that a majority of the 99 percent has benefited from the occupation of native territories.

Occupy Language might also support the campaign to stop the media from using the word "illegal" to refer to "undocumented" immigrants. From the campaign's perspective, only inanimate objects and actions are labeled illegal in English; therefore the use of "illegals" to refer to human beings is dehumanizing. As Pultizer Prize-winning journalist Jose Antonio Vargas noted in September 2012: "We must stop dehumanizing an entire group of people—actions are illegal, not people, never people. Calling people 'illegal immigrants' underscores the largely simplistic nature in which we report on and fully contextualize this issue to our readers."

The *New York Times* style-book currently asks writers to avoid terms like "illegal alien" and "undocumented," but says nothing about "illegals." Yet the *Times*' standards editor, Philip B. Corbett, weighed in on this in 2011, saying that the term "illegals" has an "unnecessarily pejorative tone" and that "it's wise to steer clear." Later in September 2012, however, he upheld the use of "illegal immigrant," citing "accuracy" for his reasoning, and ignoring the life-threatening consequences of entire groups of people.

Pejorative, discriminatory language can have real life consequences. In this case, activists worry about the coincidence of the rise in the use of the term "illegals" and the spike in hate crimes against all Latinos. As difficult as it might be to prove causation here, the National Institute for Latino Policy reports that the F.B.I.'s annual Hate Crime Statistics show that Latinos comprised *two thirds* of the victims of ethnically motivated hate crimes in 2010. When some*one* is repeatedly described as some*thing*, language has quietly paved the way for violent action.

But Occupy Language should concern itself with more than just the words we use; it should also work towards eliminating language-based racism and discrimination. In the legal system, CNN recently reported that the U.S. Justice Department alleges that Arizona's infamous Sheriff Joe Arpaio, among other offenses, has discriminated against "Latino inmates with limited English by punishing them and denying critical services." In education, as linguistic anthropologist Ana Celia Zentella notes, hostility towards those who speak "English with an accent" (Asians, Latinos, and African Americans) continues to be a problem. In housing, The National Fair Housing Alliance has long recognized "accents" as playing a significant role in housing discrimination. On the job market, language-based discrimination intersects with issues of race, ethnicity, class and national origin to make it more difficult for well-qualified applicants with an "accent" to receive equal opportunities.

In the face of such widespread language-based discrimination, Occupy Language can be a critical, progressive linguistic movement that exposes how language is used as a means of social, political and economic control. By occupying language, we can expose how educational, political, and social institutions use language to further marginalize oppressed groups; resist colonizing language practices that elevate certain language varieties over others; resist attempts to define people with terms rooted in negative stereotypes; and begin to reshape the public discourse about our communities, and about the central role of language in racism and discrimination.

Marina Sitrin and Dario Azzellini ask in their recently published book, *Occupying Language* (Zuccotti Park Press, 2012), can we, through language, advance insurgent solidarities and emancipatory social relations? As the global Occupy movement has shown, words can move entire nations of people—even the world—to action. But more than words, we must also transform the discriminatory language ideologies held by "oppressor" and "oppressed" alike.

As activist-professor Angela Davis reminded those gathered in Washington Square Park early in the Occupy movement:

We challenge language. We transform language. We remain aware of all of the resonances of the language we use…We must be aware when we say 'Occupy Wall Street' or 'Occupy Washington Square' that occupations in other countries are violent and brutal… At the same time, we transform the meaning of 'occupation'. We turn 'occupation' into something that is beautiful, something that brings community together. Something that calls for love and happiness and hope. (*Occupy: Scenes from Occupied America*, *n*+1, p. 133).

Occupy Language, as a movement, should speak to the power of language to transform how we think about the past, how we act in the present, and how we envision the future.

Thinking Big
David Palumbo-Liu

MANY OF OUR SOCIETY'S DEEPEST INEQUALITIES are presented in a series of separate and impersonal statistics. There are statistics for differences by income in home ownership, and access to employment, health care, and education. But, behind these statistics are lives and values. Even budgets, as Gladstone once remarked, are not so much matters of arithmetic, but serve as records of a society's values when we look beneath them.

In *Savage Inequalities: Children in America's Schools*, written in 1991, Jonathan Kozol attempts to bridge the distance between statistics and lives and values:[1]

In Boston, the press referred to areas like these as "death zones"—a specific reference to the rate of infant death in ghetto neighborhoods—but the feeling of the "death zone" often seemed to permeate the schools themselves... I often wondered why we would agree to let our children go to a school in places where no politician, school board president, or business CEO would dream of working. Children seemed to wrestle with these kinds of questions too. Some of their observations were, indeed, so trenchant that a teacher sometimes would step back and raise her eyebrows and then nod to me across the children's heads, as if to say, "Well, there it is! They know what's going on around them, don't they?"[2]

The simple, horrible label ("death zone") placed upon the statistic ("rates of infant death") seems to name a plain fact until we allow ourselves to question how that fact comes to be tolerated and accepted, woven into the lives of children.

Some things, unfortunately, do not change. Writing twenty years later, *The Atlantic* ran a story entitled, "Occupy Kindergarten: The Rich-Poor Divide Starts with Kindergarten."[3] In those intervening decades, the acceleration of economic inequality has intensified the disparities and despair so vividly captured in the voices found in Kozol's book.

Social science studies can deliver crisp statistics representing the proportioning of life's fortunes, but the actual substance, the reality of that monstrous disproportion, only becomes evident when we reach beyond the statistics to the people affected and confront the values that those statistics give voice to. Statistics can only represent that sliver of data that is relevant to the particular dimension of inequality being studied. What the Occupy protesters have done is to bring to the fore the interconnectedness of separate inequalities and their common, as well as distinct but interlinked, causes. The Occupy movement has raised the question of "thinking big." And fundamentally, it has made us think about the ways that "1" and "99" are not dry measures of accounting, but reflect who we are as a nation.

Let's revisit that passage from Kozol that muses that the "death zone" would never appear on the horizons of some who enjoy the freedom not to live there. The reaction to the Occupy protests from the "1%" was captured in statements such as presidential candidate Mitt Romney's dismissal of the "99%" as simply motivated by "envy" at the fortune of the deserving rich.[4] The diagnosis offered by Romney has important salience, for wealth has increasingly been seen as a virtue to which all can aspire but only the truly moral can achieve. Who wouldn't wish to have virtue? One popular bumper sticker reads, "Don't redistribute my wealth, redistribute my work ethic." Dinesh D'Souza's *The Virtue of Prosperity: Finding Values in an Age of Techno-Affluence* describes a lunch in Palo Alto with then-Forbes publisher Rich Karlgaard. D'Souza writes, "Let me assure you that Karlgaard isn't insensitive; he's a really nice guy. He cares as much as the next fellow; he just thinks that when professors such as [Michael] Walzer get started on their pet peeve of inequality, all we are getting is envy in disguise, statistical hogwash. In a word, a load of crap."[5] This flippant dismissal masks the enormous structural changes in the political economy that have transformed the United States. Such statements seek to turn the Occupy movement's value-based rejection of systematic inequality into an aggregate of individual envy.

What is needed is to think beyond isolated cases of supposed "envy," private grumblings and resentments. The issue is not haves and have-nots, but the system that so divides the lives of those two groups, the "1%" and the "99%." A movement as widespread as the Occupy movement, in its varied forms and expressions, shows that something much larger is at work. If "culture" can be viewed as embracing a common set of values, then, I would argue, a new global culture is evolving whose members are "envious" only in that they are outraged by the perpetuation of privilege and advantage in and by the hands of the few.

On November 30, 2011, two million British workers walked off the job. High inflation, cuts to social services, and a protracted period of wage stagnation will see the spending power of the average family plummet for the next five years. This sort of erosion (real median income is predicted to fall by 7 percent) has not been seen since the late 1970s. I attended a demonstration in Oxford, which drew the largest-size crowd in the southwestern part of the United Kingdom. The speeches evoked both Tahrir Square and Occupy Oakland. One woman said that up until three weeks ago she would have never imagined joining a union, and now here she was addressing a crowd of five thousand people packed into Broad Street. Not only were issues of child hunger, health care for the elderly, and education mentioned, but also the quality of the environment, access to technology, and the need for a world summit of the "99%." The message overall was that it was time to think big—this global crisis demanded a global response.

Literary and cultural studies can help us understand better how to deal with the gap between dry statistics that mask profound interconnections in the inequalities of so many lives. Consider these passages from Gabriel García Márquez's Nobel 1982 lecture, in which he speaks of statistics and the need to translate quantitative data from different worlds into our own: "Because they tried to change this state of things, nearly two hundred thousand men and women have died throughout the continent, and over one hundred thousand have lost their lives in three small and ill-fated countries of Central America: Nicaragua, El Salvador and Guatemala. If this had happened in the United States, the corresponding figure would be that of one million six hundred thousand violent deaths in four years."[6] Data needs to be set in time and place; it needs to be interpreted critically. It is literary art that can facilitate the imaginative translation of data. García Márquez finishes his lecture by stating: "I dare to think that it is this outsized reality, and not just its literary expression, that has deserved the attention of the Swedish Academy of Letters. A reality not of paper, but one that lives within us and determines each instant of our countless daily deaths, and that nourishes a source of insatiable creativity, full of sorrow and beauty, of which this roving and nostalgic Colombian is but one cipher more, singled out by fortune."[7]

This is the fiftieth anniversary of the publication of Raymond Williams's *The Long Revolution*. This work, a founding book in the cultural studies field, allows a useful, wide-frame optic onto today's Occupy protests around the world. Just as Williams' study argues forcefully for the need to think of "revolution" as a long, complex, unfolding human process, so too does he urge us to think big in a way that is imaginatively and politically capacious:

> The scale of the whole process—the struggle for democracy, the development of industry, the extension of communications, and the deep social and personal changes—is indeed too large to know or even imagine. In practice it is reduced to a series of disconnected or local changes, but while this is reasonable, in the ordinary sense, it seems to me that this scaling-down only disguises some of the deepest problems and ten-

sions, which then appear only as scattered symptoms of restlessness and uncertainty.[8]

Williams' stress falls upon the interconnectedness of politics, industry, technology, and changes in social and individual cultural life. The tendency, Williams notes, is to attempt to understand the world by rationalizing each of these aspects into their separate categories—to "scale down" (and in the academy that means, of course, political scientists on one side, engineers on another, humanists on some other part of campus, et cetera). It's not time to scale down—it's time to think, and act, big. To "identify" and hold responsible those behind the creation and perpetuation of inequality we have to see the substantive realities that underlie the statistics, and the (no longer so hidden) privileges protected by a cynical moralism and cultural stereoptypes (e.g., they are just lazy and envious). As we pursue this, we must also address the other, essential part of this struggle—to imagine the shape and scale of social change needed to disarm unfair advantage and its perpetuation of harmful in-equality. From a humanistic point of view, this means to look beyond the statistics to restore the lives and values they attest back to center stage.

ABOUT THE
CONTRIBUTORS

DAVID B. GRUSKY is Professor of Sociology at Stanford University, Director of the Center on Poverty and Inequality, coeditor of *Pathways Magazine*, and coeditor of the Stanford University Press Social Inequality Series. He is a Fellow of the American Association for the Advancement of Science, recipient of the 2004 Max Weber Award, founder of the Cornell University Center for the Study of Inequality, and a former Presidential Young Investigator.

DOUG MCADAM is Professor of Sociology at Stanford University. He is currently working on three major research projects involving the longer-term "civic effects" of the Teach for America (TFA) Program, the factors that shape county-level variation in arson attacks on churches in the U.S., and an ongoing study of neighborhood activism in Chicago between 1970-2005.

ROB REICH is Associate Professor of Political Science and, by courtesy, Philosophy, at Stanford University. He also holds a courtesy appointment in the School of Education. He is the Director of the Program on Ethics in Society and co-director of the Center on Philanthropy and Civil Society. He also has affiliations with the following programs: Urban Studies, the Haas Center for Public Service, the Clayman Institute for Gender Research, and the Center for Comparative Studies in Race and Ethnicity.

DEBRA SATZ is the Marta Sutton Weeks Professor of Ethics in Society and Professor of Philosophy at Stanford University. Prior to coming to Stanford in 1988, Dr. Satz taught at Swarthmore College. She also held fellowships at the Princeton University Center for Human Values and the Stanford Humanities Center. In 2002, she was the Marshall Weinberg Distinguished Visiting Professor at the University of Michigan. Dr. Satz grew up in the Bronx and received her B.A. from the City College of New York. She received her Ph.D. from MIT in 1987.

ERIN CUMBERWORTH is working toward her Ph.D. in Sociology at Stanford University.

KENNETH J. ARROW is an American economist and joint winner of the Nobel Memorial Prize in Economics with John Hicks in 1972.

KIM A. WEEDEN is Professor of Sociology at Cornell University. She studies inequality in advanced industrial societies, how it is organized, and how it is changing.

SEAN F. REARDON is Professor of Education and by courtesy Sociology at Stanford University, specializing in research on the effects of educational policy on educational and social inequality, on the causes, patterns, trends, and consequences of social and educational inequality, and in applied statistical methods for educational research.

PRUDENCE L. CARTER is Associate Professor of Education and (by courtesy) Sociology at Stanford University. She is also the Co-Director of the Stanford Center for Opportunity Policy in Education (SCOPE). Professor Carter teaches a range of courses on racial and ethnic relations, social and cultural inequality, the sociology of education, urban education and research methods.

SHELLEY J. CORRELL is the Barbara D. Finberg Director of the Michelle R. Clayman Institute for Gender Research at Stanford University. She is also a professor in the department of sociology at Stanford and an active member of the American Sociological Association.

GARY SEGURA is a Professor of American Politics and Chair of Chicano/a Studies in the Center for Comparative Studies in Race and Ethnicity at Stanford University. He is also a principal in the polling firm Latino Decisions™. His work focuses on issues of political representation, and the politics to America's growing Latino minority.

DAVID D. LAITIN is the James T. Watkins IV and Elise V. Watkins Professor of Political Science at Stanford University. He received his BA from Swarthmore College, and then served as a Peace Corps Volunteer in Somalia and Grenada, where he became national tennis champion in 1970. Back in the US, he received his Ph.D. in political science from UC Berkeley, working under the direction of Ernst Haas and Hanna Pitkin.

CRISTOBAL YOUNG is Assistant Professor in the Department of Sociology at Stanford University.

CHARLES VARNER is a graduate student in Sociology at Princeton University. He interested in patterns of social stratification and inequality. He studies the effects of racial and ethnic heterogeneity on both individual attitudes and broader social policy outcomes.

PAUL R. EHRLICH received his Ph.D. from the University of Kansas. Co-founder with Peter H. Raven of the field of coevolution, he has pursued long-term studies of the structure, dynamics, and genetics of natural butterfly populations. He has also been a pioneer in alerting the public to the problems of overpopulation, and in raising issues of population, resources, and the environment as matters of public policy.

ANNE H. EHRLICH is Policy Coordinator at the Center for Conservation Biology at Stanford University. She is co-author (with her husband Paul R. Ehrlich), most recently, of *The Dominant Animal: Human Evolution and the Environment.*

DONALD A. BARR is Associate Professor of Pediatrics at Stanford University. He is the author of *Introduction to U.S. Health Policy*, and *Health Disparities in the United States*, both published by Johns Hopkins.

MICHELE ELAM is the Olivier Nomellini Family University Fellow in Undergraduate Education and Martin Luther King, Jr. Centennial Professor in the Department of English at Stanford University, and the author of two books on race and culture, including most recently *The Souls of Mixed Folk: Race, Politics and Aesthetics in the New Millennium* (2011).

JENNIFER DEVERE BRODY is an Affiliate in the Center for Comparative Studies of Race and Ethnicity at Stanford where she Chairs the Department of Theater and Performance Studies. She has written two books and her research in the fields of race and sexuality by the Ford Foundation and the Monette/Horwitz Trust for Independent Research against Homophobia.

H. SAMY ALIM is Associate Professor of Education and (by courtesy) Anthropology and Linguistics at Stanford University, where he directs the Center for Race, Ethnicity, and Language (CREAL) and the Institute for Diversity in the Arts (IDA). His most recent book *Articulate While Black: Barack Obama, Language, and Race in the US* (Oxford University Press, 2012, with Geneva Smitherman) examines American racial politics through the lens of language.

DAVID PALUMBO-LIU is Professor and Director of Comparative Literature at Stanford University, and author, most recently, of *The Deliverance of Others: Reading Literature in a Global Age* (forthcoming).

Notes

II. The Empirical and Normative Foundation

David B. Grusky and Erin Cumberworth

[1] It is possible to further reduce the amount of inequality by taking into account the cost of health care coverage from Medicare, Medicaid, and employer-provided insurance (see Richard V. Burkhauser, Jeff Larrimore, and Kosali Simon. "A Second Opinion on the Economic Health of the American Middle Class and Why it Matters in Gauging the Impact of Government Policy." National Tax Journal 65 (March): 7-32). Although this approach increases the share of income going to the bottom and middle of the income distribution, it still reveals healthy increases in inequality over the period from 1979 to 2007.

[2] Atkinson, Anthony B., Thomas Piketty, and Emmanuel Saez. 2011. "Top Incomes in the Long Run of History." Journal of Economic Literature 49:1, pp. 3-71.

[3] The data have been assembled by the Economic Policy Institute (see http://stateofworkingamerica.org).

[4] Emmanuel Saez. 2012. "Striking it Richer: The Evolution of Top Incomes in the United States," Updated version of manuscript originally published in Pathways Magazine, 2008, available at http://elsa.berkeley.edu/~saez/.

[5] Kopczuk, Wojciech, and Emmanuel Saez. 2004. "Top Wealth Shares in the United States, 1916-2000: Evidence from Estate Tax Returns," National Tax Journal, Vol. LVII, No. 2, Part 2, June, pp. 445-87. The updated results are available at http://elsa.berkeley.edu/~saez/TabFig2008.xls.

[6] Wolff, Edward N., Lindsay A. Owens, and Esra Burak. 2011. "How Much Wealth Was Destroyed in the Great Recession?" Pp. 127-158 in David B. Grusky, Bruce Western, and Christopher Wimer, eds., The Great Recession. New York: Russell Sage Foundation.

[7] Piketty, Thomas, and Emmanuel Saez. 2003. "Income Inequality in the United States, 1913-1998." Quarterly Journal of Economics 118, No. 1 (February), pp. 1-39.

[8] This is the very persuasive line of argumentation pushed by Wojciech Kopczuk and Emmanuel Saez (see endnote 5).

[9] Anthony B. Atkinson, Thomas Piketty, and Emmanuel Saez. 2011. "Top Incomes in the Long Run of History." Journal of Economic Literature 49:1, pp. 3-71. See also Anthony B. Atkinson and Thomas Piketty. 2007. Top Incomes over the Twentieth Century: A Contrast between Continental European and English-Speaking Countries. Oxford and New York: Oxford University Press.

[10] Congressional Budget Office. 2011. Trends in the Distribution of Household Income Between 1979 and 2007. For a discussion of the changing effects of taxes and transfers, see pages 35-47 in particular. http://cbo.gov/publication/42729

[11] For a pathbreaking discussion of this moral economy effect, see Bruce Western and Jake Rosenfeld, 2011, "Unions, Norms, and the Rise in U.S. Wage Inequality," American Sociological Review 76, pp. 513-37.

[12] For a discussion of deunionization in the United States, see Jake Rosenfeld, 2010, "Little Labor: How Union Decline is Changing the American Landscape," 2011, Pathways Magazine, Summer 2010. http://www.stanford.edu/group/scspi/media_magazines_pathways_summer_2010.html.

[13] Bruce Western and Jake Rosenfeld. 2011. "Unions, Norms, and the Rise in U.S. Wage Inequality." American Sociological Review 76, pp. 513-37.

[14] The income data pertain to the hourly wages of full-time private-sector males, while inequality is measured here as the variance of log wages within groups defined by age, race, ethnicity, education, region, union membership, and region-industry unionization rates. The corresponding results for between-group inequality show very little effect of unionization.

[15] This estimate, which includes the "normative effects" of unions, is rather larger than that secured by other scholars (e.g., David Card, 2001, "The Effect of Unions on the Structure of Wages: A Longitudinal Analysis," Econometrica 64, pp. 957-79).

[16] These figures come from the Economic Policy Institute and pertain to total direct compensation (for CEOs).

[17] For a review of the relevant literature, see Robert J. Gordon and Ian Dew-Becker, 2007, "Selected Issues in the Rise of Income Inequality," Brookings Papers on Economic Activity, no. 2 (Fall 2007), pp. 169–190. Also see Pathways Magazine, Summer 2010, http://www.stanford.edu/group/scspi/media_magazines_pathways_summer_2010.html.

[18] Goldin, Claudia, and Lawrence Katz, 2008, The Race Between Education and Technology, Cambridge: Harvard University Press; Autor, David H., Lawrence F. Katz, and Melissa S. Kearney, 2008, The Review of Economics and Statistics, 90(2), pp. 300-323; Grusky, David B., and Kim A. Weeden. 2011. "Is Market Failure Behind the Takeoff in Inequality?" Pp. 90-97 in The Inequality Reader: Contemporary and Foundational Readings in Race, Class, and Gender, 2nd Edition, edited by David B. Grusky and Szonja Szelényi. Boulder: Westview Press.

[19] Kopczuk, Wojciech, and Emmanuel Saez. 2004. "Top Wealth Shares in the United States, 1916-2000: Evidence from Estate Tax Returns," National Tax Journal, Vol. LVII, No. 2, Part 2, June, pp. 445-87.

Rob Reich and Debra Satz

[1] 400 wealthiest Americans: http://www.politifact.com/wisconsin/statements/2011/mar/10/michael-moore/michael-moore-says-400-americans-have-more-wealth-/

Between 1979 and 2007...: http://www.cbo.gov/ftpdocs/124xx/doc12485/10-25-HouseholdIncome.pdf

Short summary here: http://cboblog.cbo.gov/?p=2909

According to newly released measures: http://www.nytimes.com/interactive/2011/11/19/us/bordering-on-poverty.html

Link to the Census Report: http://www.census.gov/prod/2011pubs/p60-241.pdf

[2] Economic Mobility: Is the American Dream Alive and Well? See page 5 http://www.economicmobility.org/assets/pdfs/EMP%20American%20Dream%20Report.pdf

[3] US Dept of Education, National Center for Education Statistics, 2009.

[4] Left Behind: Unequal Opportunity in Higher Education. http://tcf.org/media-center/pdfs/pr19/leftbehindrc.pdf

[5] Percentage of Congress who are millionaires: http://www.opensecrets.org/news/2011/11/congress-enjoys-robust-financial-status.html

[6] Thomas Piketty and Emmanuel Saez, "How Progressive is the U.S. Federal Tax System? A Historical and International Perspective," Journal of Economic Perspectives, Vol. 21, No. 1, Winter 2007: 3-24. http://elsa.berkeley.edu/~saez/piketty-saezJEP07taxprog.pdf

[7] This paragraph is indebted to arguments made by Alan Krueger, Princeton economist and chair of the Council of Economic

Advisers, in a January 2012 speech to the Center for American Progress. http://www.whitehouse.gov/sites/default/files/krueger_cap_speech_final_remarks.pdf

III. The Sources of the Takeoff

Kenneth J. Arrow

[1] http://www.census.gov/hhes/www/income/data/historical/people

[2] U. S. Census website

[3] Ibid.

[4] Facundo Alvarado, Anthony Atkinson, Thomas Piketty, and Emmanuel Saez, "The World Top Incomes Database." http://g-mond.parisschoolofeconomics.eu/topincomes/

[5] Computed from the data in Darien B. Jacobson, Brien G. Raub, and Barry W. Johnson "The Estate Tax: Ninety Years and Counting." http://www.irs.gov/pub/irs-soi/ninetyestate.pdf.

[6] Current employment Statistics Survey, U.S. Bureau of Labor Statistics, http://data.bls.gov/timeseries/ES3000000001?data_tool=XGtable.

[7] http://unionstats.gsu.edu/Privat%20Sectdor%20workers.xls

[8] Computed from U.A. Bureau of Economic Analysis, NIPA Table 6.16, http://www.bea.gov/national/nipaweb.

David B. Grusky and Kim A. Weeden

[1] These statistics pertain to the new Supplemental Poverty Measure. Tritch, Teresa. 2011. "Reading Between the Poverty Lines," New York Times, November 19, 2011 (see http://www.nytimes.com/2011/11/20/opinion/sunday/reading-between-the-poverty-lines.html?_r=2).

[2] Konczal, Mike. 2011. "How Killer Student Debt and Unemployment Made Young People the Leaders at Occupy Wall Street"(see http://www.alternet.org/newsandviews/article/675403/how_killer_student_debt_and_unemployment_made_young_people_the_leaders_at_occupy_wall _street).

[3] Goldin, Claudia, and Lawrence F. Katz. (2008). The Race Between Education and Technology. Cambridge, MA: Harvard University Press.

[4] Burtless, G., & Gordon, T. (2011). The federal stimulus programs and their effects." In D. B. Grusky, B. Western, & C. Wimer (Eds.), The Great Recession (pp. 249–293). New York: Russell Sage Foundation.

IV. Who Bears the Brunt of the Takeoff?

Sean F. Reardon

[1] Thomas Piketty and Emmanuel Saez, *Income Inequality in the United States*, 1913-1998 (Tables and figures updated to 2008), 2010. Retrieved 19 October 2011 from http://www.econ.berkeley.edu/~saez/TabFig2008.xls.

[2] Sean F. Reardon, "The widening socioeconomic status achieve-

ment gap: New evidence and possible explanations," in *Whither Opportunity? Rising Inequality and the Uncertain Life Chances of Low-Income Children*, ed. R. J. Murnane & G. J. Duncan (New York: Russell Sage Foundation, 2011).

[3] Alexander W. Astin and Leticia Oseguera, L., "The Declining 'Equity' of American Higher Education," *The Review of Higher Education* 27(3) (2004): 321-341; Martha J. Bailey and Susan M. Dynarski, "Gains and Gaps: A Historical Perspective on Inequality in College Entry and Completion," in *Whither Opportunity? Rising Inequality and the Uncertain Life Chances of Low-Income Children*; Philippe Belley and Lance Lochner, "The changing role of family income and ability in determining educational achievement," *National Bureau of Economic Research Working Paper 13527*.

[4] David H. Autor, Lawrence F. Katz, L. H., and Melissa S. Kearney, "Trends in U.S. Wage Inequality: Revising the Revisionists," *The Review of Economics and Statistics* 90(2) (2008): 300-323; Richard J. Murnane, John B. Willett, and Frank Levy, F., "The Growing Importance of Cognitive Skills in Wage Determination," *The Review of Economics and Statistics*, 78(2) (1995): 251-266.

[5] Katharine Bradbury, "Trends in U.S. Family Income Mobility, 1969–2006," *Federal Reserve Bank of Boston Working Paper, 11-10* (2011).

[6] Reardon, "The widening socioeconomic status achievement gap: New evidence and possible explanations."

[7] Paul A. Jargowsky, "Take the money and run: Economic segregation in U.S. metropolitan areas," *American Sociological Review*

61(6) (1996): 984-998; Sean F. Reardon and Kendra Bischoff, *Growth in the residential segregation of families by income,* 1970-2009 (2011); Sean F. Reardon and Kendra Bischoff, "Income Inequality and Income Segregation," *American Journal of Sociology* 116(4) (2011): 1092-1153; Tara Watson, T., "Inequality and the Measurement of Residential Segregation by Income," *Review of Income and Wealth* 55(3) (2009): 820-844.

[8] Jonathan Guryan, Erik Hurst, and Melissa Kearney, "Parental Education and Parental Time with Children," *Journal of Economic Perspectives* 22(3) (2008): 23-46; Sabino Kornrich and Frank Furstenberg, "Investing in Children: Changes in Parental Spending on Children, 1972 to 2007," *Demography* (forthcoming); Gary Ramey and Valerie A. Ramey, "The rug rat race," *National Bureau of Economic Research Working Paper 15284.*

[9] First Focus, "Big Ideas For Children: Investing in Our Nation's Future," available from http://www.firstfocus.net/library/reports/big-ideas-investing-our-nations-future (2008); see also www.heckmanequation.org.

Prudence L. Carter

[1] Ira Katznelson, *When Affirmative Action Was White: An Untold History of Racial Inequality in Twentieth-Century America.* New York: W.W. Norton & Company, 2006.

[2] Ibid.

[3] Retrieved online at http://iasp.brandeis.edu/pdfs/Racial-Wealth-Gap-Brief.pdf on December 1, 2011.

[4] Retrieved online at http://www.pewsocialtrends.org/2011/07/26/wealth-gaps-rise-to-record-highs-between-whites-blacks-hispanics/ on December 1, 2011.

[5] Bureau of Labor Statistics, 2011. Retrieved online at http://www.bls.gov/opub/ted/2011/ted_20111005.htm on February 13, 2012.

[6] Retrieved online at http://www.nytimes.com/2011/11/29/us/as-public-sector-sheds-jobs-black-americans-are-hit-hard.html on December 1, 2011.

[7] Linda Darling-Hammond. *The Flat World and Education: How America's Commitment to Equity Will Determine Our Future*. New York: Teachers College Press, 2010.

[8] Angelina KewalRamani, Lauren Gilbertson, Mary Ann Fox, and Stephen Provasnik. 2007. "Status and Trends in the Education of Racial and Ethnic Minorities (NCES 2007-039)." Washington, D.C.: National Center for Education Statistics, Institute of Education Sciences, U.S. Department of Education.

[9] Amy J. Orr. "Black-White Differences in Achievement: The Importance of Wealth." *Sociology of Education* 76 (2003):281-304.

Christopher Jencks and Meredith Phillips. Eds. *The Black-White Test Score Gap*. Washington, D.C.: Brookings Institution Press, 1998.

[10] Gary Orfield, 2009. "Reviving the Goal of an Integrated Society: A 21st Century Challenge." In UCLA Civil Rights Project,

accessed November 18, 2011. http://civilrightsproject.ucla.edu/ research/k-12-education/integration-and-diversity/reviving-the-goal-of-an-integrated-society-a-21st-century-challenge/orfield-reviving-the-goal-mlk-2009.pdf

[11] Prudence L. Carter, *Stubborn Roots: Race, Culture, and Inequality in U.S. & South African Schools*. New York: Oxford University Press, 2012; Karolyn Tyson, Integration Interrupted: Tracking, Black Students, and Acting White after Brown. New York, Oxford University Press, 2011; Amanda Lewis, *Race in the Schoolyard: Reproducing the Color Line in School*. New Brunswick, NJ: Rutgers University Press, 2003; Roslyn Arlin Mickelson. "Subverting Swann: First- and Second-Generation Segregation in the Charlotte-Mecklenburg Schools." *American Educational Research Journal* (2001) 38:215-252.

[12] NAACP Legal Defense and Educational Fund, 2006. Dismantling the school-to-prison pipeline. Retrieved March 23, 2009, from http://www.naacpldf.org/content/pdf/pipeline/Dismantling_the_School_to_Prison_Pipeline.pdf

[13] Douglas Massey and Nancy Denton. *American Apartheid*. Cambridge: Harvard University Press, 1993; Kenneth Arrow. "What Has Economics to Say about Racial Discrimination?" *The Journal of Economic Perspectives* 12 (1998):91-100; William Darity, Jr. and Samuel L Myers, Jr. *Persistent Disparity: Racial and Economic Inequality in the United States since 1945*. Northampton, MA: Edward Elgar Publishers, 1998.

[14] Mica Pollock. *Colormute: Race Talk Dilemmas in an American School*. Princeton, NJ: Princeton University Press, 2004.

Shelley J. Correll

[1] Wojciech, Kopczuk, Emanuel Saez and Jae Song, "Earnings inequality and Mobility in the United States: Evidence from social security data since 1937," *The Quarterly Review of Economics.* February (2010): Figure 10, 122.

[2] Forbes Staff, "The richest people in America, *The Forbes 400*, Forbes, January 30, 2012.

[3] Fowler, Meg, "From Eisenhower to Obama: What the wealthiest Americans pay in Taxes," ABC News, January 18, 2012, accessed February 12, 2012, http://news.yahoo.com/eisenhower-obama-wealthiest-americans-pay-taxes-193734550--abc-news.html . See also Department of Treasury, Office of Tax Analysis, December 30, 2010, "Capital gains and taxes paid on capital gains for returns with positive net capital gains, 1954-2008."

[4] World Bank, *Monitoring Environmental Progress*, Washington D.C., 1995. (See chapter 8).

[5] Gary S. Becker and Nigel Tomas, "Human capital and the rise and fall of families," *Journal of Labor Economics* 43 (1994), 209.

[6] Duncan Ironmonger, "Counting outputs, capital inputs, and caring labor: Estimating gross household products," *Feminist Economics* 2 (1996), 149.

[7] Landefeld, J. Steven and Stephanie H. McCulla, "Accounting for nonmarket household production within a national accounts framework," *Review of Income and Wealth* 46 (2000): 289–307.

[8] Youngjoo Cha, "Reinforcing separate spheres: The effect of spousal overwork on the employment of men and women in dual earner households, *American Sociological Review* 75 (2010) 303-329.

[9] Youngjoo Cha and Kim Weeden, "Overwork and the slow convergence of the gender wage gap," Paper presented at the American Sociological Association annual meeting, Las Vegas, NV, August 2011.

[10] Schmeichel, Brandon J., Kathleen D. Vohs and Roy F. Baumeister, "Intellectual performance and ego depletion: Role of self in the logical reasoning and other information processing," *Journal of Personality and Social Psychology*, 85 (2003), 33-46.

[11] Vohs, Kathleen D., Roy F. Buarmeister, Brandon J. Schmeichel, Jean M. Twenge, Noelle M. Nelson and Dianne M. Tice, "Making choices impairs subsequent self-control: A limited resource account of decision-making, self-regulation, and active initiative, *Journal of Personality and Social Psychology* 94 (2008), 883-898.

[12] Families and Work Institute, *Overwork in America: When the Way We Work Becomes Too Much*, 2005.

[13] Youngjoo Cha. "Gender Inequality in Overworking America," (PhD Dissertation, Cornell University, 2010), 33-34.

[14] Jukiesch, Michael K. and Karen S. Lyness, "Left behind? The impact of leaves of absences on managers' career success," *Academy of Management Journal* 42 (1999), 641, 648.

[15] Manchester, Collen F., Lisa M. Leslie and Amit Kramer. "Stop the clock policies and career success in academia, *American Economic Review: Papers & Proceedings* 100 (2010) 219-223.

[16] Bianchi, Suzanne, "Family change and time allocation in American families," Workplace Flexibility 2010 conference, Washington D.C. November 29-30, 2010.

V. Inequality, Politics, and Democracy

Gary Segura

[1] Fukuyama, Francis. 1992. *The End of History and the Last Man*. New York: Free Press.

[2] Fukuyama, Francis. 1989. "The End of History?" *The National Interest*, Summer.

[3] Rakoff, Jed. 2011. *U.S. Securities and Exchange Commission v. Citigroup Global Markets, Inc.* 11 Civ. 7387 (JSR), Opinion and Order.

[4] Taibbi, Matt. 2011. "Federal Judge Pimp-Slaps the SEC Over Citigroup Settlement," *Rolling Stone* online, November 29, 10:10 am. http://www.rollingstone.com/politics/blogs/taibblog/federal-judge-pimp-slaps-the-sec-over-citigroup-settlement-20111129

[5] Rakoff, Jed. 2011. *U.S. Securities and Exchange Commission v. Citigroup Global Markets, Inc.* 11 Civ. 7387 (JSR), Opinion and Order, p. 10.

[6] Teitelbaum, Richard. 2011. "How Paulson Gave Hedge Funds Advance Word of Fannie Mae Rescue," *Bloomberg Markets Magazine* online, posted November 29, 12:46 pm. http://www.bloomberg.com/news/2011-11-29/how-henry-paulson-gave-hedge-funds-advance-word-of-2008-fannie-mae-rescue.html

[7] Schmidt, Julie. 2012. "Feds, states, banks agree to mortgage settlement." *USA Today*, February 9. http://www.usatoday.com/money/story/2012-02-08/states-mortgage-settlement/53016420/1

[8] Andrews, Edmund L. 2008. "Greenspan concedes error on regulation." *New York Times*, October 23. http://www.nytimes.com/2008/10/24/business/economy/24panel.html?_r=2

[9] Saez, Emmanuel. 2012. "Striking it Richer: The Evolution of Top Incomes in the United States." http://elsa.berkeley.edu/~saez/saez-UStopincomes-2010.pdf

[10] http://www.opensecrets.org/pres08/contrib.php?cid=N00009638

David D. Laitin

[1] Duncan Black (1948) "On the rationale of group decision-making", Journal of Political Economy 56: 23–34. Because the median voter is an abstraction, I present it as a de-gendered "it".

[2] Note well from this example that the preferred tax rate for our destitute citizen's would be 14/15 of all income to be redistributed, and the high flyer would prefer no taxes at all for redistribution.

[3] For census data, see http://www.census.gov/hhes/www/income/data/historical/household/.

[4] For data on marginal tax rates, see http://ntu.org/tax-basics/history-of-federal-individual-1.html

[5] The classic paper demonstrating this is A. H. Meltzer and S. F. Richard (1981) "A Rational Theory of the Size of Government", Journal of Political Economy, 89: 914–927

[6] http://www.dol.gov/whd/minwage/chart.htm

[7] For a discussion of the geography of inequality, see Tiberiu Dragu and Jonathan Rodden "Representation and Redistribution in Federations" Proceedings of the National Academy of Sciences

[8] For a defense of this radical proposal, see John Mark Hansen (2008) "Equal Voice by Half Measures", First Impressions the online companion to the Michigan Law Review 106(4): 100-104.

[9] See Thomas W. Hiltachk (2008) "Reforming the Electoral College One State at a Time" First Impressions the online companion to the Michigan Law Review 106(4): 90-94.

[10] On the National Popular Vote bill see http://www.national-popularvote.com/

[11] For an assessment of the electoral impact of felon disenfranchisement, see Jeff Manza and Christopher Uggen (2006) Locked Out: Felon Disenfranchisement and American Democracy (New York: Oxford University Press).

[12] This section relies on the analyses in Nolan McCarty, Keith T. Poole, and Howard Rosenthal (2006) Polarized America (Cambridge: MIT Press)

[13] Alexander Keyssar (2000) The Right to Vote (New York: Basic Books)

[14] Exemplified in Thomas Frank (2004) What's the Matter with Kansas? (New York: Henry Holt).

[15] Larry M. Bartels (2008) Unequal Democracy (Princeton: Princeton University Press)

Cristobal Young & Charles Varner

[1] Robert H. Frank, and Phillip J. Cook. *The Winner-Take-All Society: how more and more Americans compete for ever fewer and bigger prizes, encouraging economic waste, income inequality, and an impoverished cultural life.* New York: Free Press (1995).

[2] Thomas Piketty and Emmanuel Saez. "Income Inequality in the United States, 1913-1998." *Quarterly Journal of Economics*, Vol. 118(2003). See also, Emmanuel Saez, "Striking it Richer: The Evolution of Top Incomes in the United States." *Pathways,* Winter (2008), updated to 2010 at http://elsa.berkeley.edu/~saez/ TabFig2010.xls (Table A3). In 2007, the income share of the top 1 percent stood at 23.5 percent – the highest recorded since 1928. After a drop during the most recent recession, the income share of the top 1 percent is growing again: in the first year of the economic recovery (2010), the top 1 percent captured 93 percent of total income growth in the economy (Table 1).

[3] Gary Langer, ABC News/Washington Post Poll, September 29–October 2, 2011, http://www.langerresearch.com/ uploads/1128a3Politics.pdf.

[4] OECD Tax Database 2010. "Personal Income Tax Rates and Thresholds for Central Governments." http://www.oecd.org/

dataoecd/43/63/1942474.xls

5 The traditional definition of a millionaire is to have $1 million or more in net wealth. Since income taxes do not apply to wealth, the popular application of the term is technically incorrect. Nevertheless, in the high end of the income distribution, most people's net wealth is greater than their annual income. For example, Mitt Romney's annual income in 2010 was $21.6 million, but his net wealth is estimated at $250 million. In America on average, household wealth is five times household income (Ergungor and Waiwood, 2011).

6 Steve Stanek, "Md. Millionaires Hit by Tax Bracket for Wealthy," *Budget and Tax News*, July 2008, http://heartland.org/issue-archive/budget-and-tax-news.

7 Office of the Governor, "Remarks of Governor Chris Christie to the Joint Session of the New Jersey Senate and General Assembly Regarding the Fiscal Year 2011 Budget," March 16, 2010, http://www.state.nj.us/governor/news/addresses/2010s/approved/20100316.html.

8 Cristobal Young and Charles Varner. "Millionaire Migration and State Taxation of Top Incomes: Evidence from a Natural Experiment." *National Tax Journal*. Vol. 64(2011).

9 Raven Malloy, Christopher Smith, and Abigail Wozniak. "Internal Migration in the United States." *Journal of Economic Perspectives*. Vol. 25(2011).

10 The exact trigger points for the tax would be designed so that the tax would average 3 percent over the business cycle, based on the state's usual unemployment rates. State unemployment

insurance benefits are already structured this way, to provide temporary extra benefits during recessions.

[11] Estimate from the Center of Budget and Policy Priorities. http://www.cbpp.org/cms/index.cfm?fa=view&id=711

Doug McAdam

[1] Cathy Cohen, *Democracy Remixed*, Oxford University Press, 2010.

VI. The Social Costs of Inequality

Paul R. Ehrlich & Anne H. Ehrlich

[1] William Rees, "What's blocking sustainability? Human nature, cognition, and denial," *Sustainability: Science, Practice, & Policy* 6 (2010): 13-25; Naomi Oreskes and Erik M. Conway, *Merchants of Doubt* (New York: Bloomsbury Press, 2010).

[2] Donella H. Meadows et al. *The Limits to Growth* (Washington, DC: Universe Books, 1972).

[3] Charles A. S. Hall and John W. Day Jr., "Revisiting the limits to growth after peak oil," *American Scientist* 97 (2009): 230-237.

[4] Mathis Wackernagel et al., "Tracking the ecological overshoot of the human economy," *Proceedings of the National Academy of Sciences USA* 99 (2002): 9266-9271; Rees, "What's blocking sustainability?"

[5] Gretchen C. Daily, ed., *Nature's Services: Societal Dependence on Natural Ecosystems* (Washington, DC: Island Press, 1997).

[6] Paul R. Ehrlich and Anne H. Ehrlich, *The Dominant Animal: Human Evolution and the Environment*, Second Edition (Washington, DC: Island Press, 2009).

[7] Intergovernmental Panel on Climate Change (IPCC), "Climate Change 2007: The Physical Science Basis," Summary for Policymakers, contribution of Working Group I to the Fourth Assessment Report (Geneva, Switzerland: IPCC Secretariat, 2007); James Hansen et al., "Target atmospheric CO2: Where should humanity aim?", *The Open Atmospheric Science Journal* 2 (2008): 217-231.

[8] Paul R. Ehrlich and Anne H. Ehrlich, "The culture gap and its needed closures," *International Journal of Environmental Studies* 67 (2010): 481-492.

[9] John Harte, "Human population as a dynamic factor in environmental degradation," *Population and Environment* 28 (2007): 223-236.

[10] IPCC, "Climate Change 2007."

[11] IPCC, "Climage Change 2007."

[12] Owen B. Toon et al., "Consequences of regional-scale nuclear conflicts," *Science* 315 (2007): 1224-1225.k.

[13] Ehrlich and Ehrlich, *The Dominant Animal*; Daily, *Nature's Services*.

[14] Gretchen C. Daily and Paul R. Ehrlich, "Global change and human susceptibilty to disease," *Annual Review of Energy and the Environment* 21 (1996): 125-144.

[15] Ehrlich and Ehrlich, *The Dominant Animal.*

[16] Carl Haub and James Gribble, "The world at 7 billion," *Population Bulletin* 66:2 (Washington, DC: Population Reference Bureau, 2011); Population Action International, "Why Population Matters" (Washington, DC, 2011).

[17] Johan Rockström et al., "Planetary boundaries: exploring the safe operating space for humanity," Ecology and Society 14:32 (2009). Available at http://www.ecologyandsociety.org/vol14/iss32/art32/

Donald A. Barr

[1] Kaiser Family Foundation and Health Research and Education Trust. Employer Health Benefits 2010 Annual Survey, Summary of Findings, p. 1, available at http://ehbs.kff.org/2010.html, accessed 2/14/12.

[2] The Commonwealth Fund. State Trends in Premiums and Deductibles, 2003–2010: The Need for Action to Address Rising Costs. November, 2011, p. 6, available at http://www.commonwealthfund.org/Publications/Issue-Briefs/2011/Nov/State-Trends-in-Premiums.aspx, accessed 2/14/12.

[3] Rand Corporation. Rand Health Research Highlights. How Does Growth in Health Care Costs Affect the American Family?, p. 2,

available at http://www.rand.org/pubs/research_briefs/RB9605. html, accessed 2/14/12.

[4] Newhouse, JP, WG Manning, CN Morris, et al. Some Interim Results From a Controlled Trial of Cost Sharing in Health Insurance. New England Journal of Medicine 1981; 305:1501-07.

[5] Haviland, Amelia M, Neeraj Sood, Roland McDevitt, and M. Susan Marquis. How Do Consumer-Directed Health Plans Affect Vulnerable Populations? Forum for Health Economics & Policy. April, 2011. 14(2): 1–23, ISSN (Online) 1558-9544, DOI: 10.2202/1558-9544.1248.

[6] Galbraith, Alison A., Stephen B. Soumerai, Dennis Ross-Degnan, Meredith B. Rosenthal, Charlene Gay and Tracy A. Lieu1. Delayed and Forgone Care for Families with Chronic Conditions in High-Deductible Health Plans. Journal of General Internal Medicine. Published online: 18 January 2012. DOI: 10.1007/s11606-011-1970-8.

[7] Kaiser Family Foundation and Health Research and Education Trust. Employer Health Benefits 2010 Annual Survey, Summary of Findings, p. 1, available at http://ehbs.kff.org/2010.html, accessed 2/14/12.

[8] Center for American Progress Action Fund. Health Care in Crisis: 14,000 Losing Coverage Each Day. February 19, 2009, available at http://www.americanprogressaction.org/issues/2009/02/health_in_crisis.html, accessed 2/14/12.

[9] Holahan, John and Vicki Chen. Changes in Health Insurance Coverage in the Great Recession, 2007-2010. December 2011, available at http://www.kff.org/uninsured/upload/8264.pdf, accessed 2/14/12.

[10] Woolf, Steven H. and Paula Braveman. Where Health Disparities Begin: The Role Of Social And Economic Determinants—And Why Current Policies May Make Matters Worse. Health Affairs. 2011; 30(10): 1852-1859.

[11] U.S. Center for Disease Control and Prevention. Prevalence of Coronary Heart Disease—United States, 2006—2010. Morbidity and Mortality Weekly Report. October 14, 2011. 60(40): 1377-138.

[12] Alter, David A, Therese Stukel, Alice Chong, and David Henry. Lesson From Canada's Universal Care: Socially Disadvantaged Patients Use More Health Services, Still Have Poorer Health. Health Affairs. 2011; 30(2): 274-83.

[13] Whitehall II - Stress and Health Study. University College London, Research Department of Epidemiology And Public Health. http://www.ucl.ac.uk/whitehallII/, accessed 4/11/12.

[14] Woolf, Steven H. and Paula Braveman. Where Health Disparities Begin: The Role Of Social And Economic Determinants—And Why Current Policies May Make Matters Worse. Health Affairs. 2011; 30(10): 1852-1859.

[15] Ibid.

VII. Inequality and Culture

Michele Elam & Jennifer DeVere Brody

[1] Audre Lorde, "Poetry is not a luxury," in Sister Outsider: Essays and Speeches (Berkeley, Ca.: Crossing Press, 1984): 36-39.

[2] On Occupy art and race, see also Michele Elam, "How Art Propels Wall Street," http://www.cnn.com/2011/11/01/opinion/elam-occupy-art/

[3] Author anonymous. This image joins a growing folk gallery of over a thousand other largely unattributed "Sargent Pike memes." See http://knowyourmeme.com/memes/casually-pepper-spray-everything-cop/photos?fb_ref=recommendations_memes. Last accessed March 12, 2012.

[4] Wikimedia Commons. http://commons.wikimedia.org/wiki/Main_Page. Last accessed March 12, 2012.

[5] Ben Davis, "Why I Support the Occupy Museums Protesters, and Why You Should Too," Blouin Artinfo, Online International Edition (October 26, 2011). http://www.artinfo.com/news/story/449610/ben-davis-why-i-support-occupy-museums-protesters-and-why-you-should-too

[6] Yayoi Kusama, Press Release, "Wall Street Anatomic Explosion," New York. Fall 1968. Blanton Archive, University of Texas at Austin.

[7] See, for instance, W.E.B. Du Bois, "Criteria of Negro Art" (1926) in The Oxford W.E.B. Du Bois Reader, ed. Eric J. Sundquist (NY: Oxford University Press, 1996): 993-1002.

[8] Juliet Fleming, Graffiti and the Writing Arts of Early Modern England. (Philadelphia,PA: University of Pennsylvania Press, 2001).

H. Samy Alim

[1] http://www.americandialect.org/occupy-is-the-2011-word-of-the-year

David Palumbo-Liu

[1] New York: Harper Perennial ed, 1992. Originally published New York: Crown, 1991.

[2] Kozol, 5.

[3] By Jordan Weissmann: http://www.theatlantic.com/business/archive/2012/02/occupy-kindergarten-the-rich-poor-divide-starts-with-education/252914/#.Tzr4m7wmsTE.email

[4] Greg Sargent, "Romney: Questions about Wall Street and Inequality Driven by 'Envy'," *Washington Post* 11 January 2012: http://www.washingtonpost.com/blogs/plum-line/post/romney-questions-about-wall-street-and-inequality-are-driven-by-envy/2012/01/11/gIQAJ6L2qP_blog.html

[5] Dinesh D'Souza, *The Virtue of Prosperity* (New York and London: The Free Press, 2000), 69.

[6] Gabriel García Márquez, "The Solitude of Latin America." Nobel prize speech, 8 December 1982. <http://nobelprize.org/nobel_prizes/literature/laureates/1982/marquez-lecture.html>.

[7] García Márquez, op cit.

[8] *The Long Revolution.* New York: Columbia University Press, 1961; rpt Cardigan, Wales: Parthian Press, 2011 with a foreword by Anthony Barnett, page 12.

BOSTON REVIEW BOOKS

Boston Review Books is an imprint of *Boston Review*, a bimonthly magazine of ideas. The book series, like the magazine, covers a lot of ground. But a few premises tie it all together: that democracy depends on public discussion; that sometimes understanding means going deep; that vast inequalities are unjust; and that human imagination breaks free from neat political categories. Visit bostonreview.net for more information.